Dedication

I dedicate this book to my wife, Renee, and our three children, Andrea, Richard, and Robert.

CONTENTS

FOREWORD

Youth gangs which are active in crime are not new. They have always existed. During the industrial revolution they were rooted in the migration to cities where they survived off pillage and thievery. They were the result of urban decay, poverty, discrimination, family disorganization, cultural differences, social class resentments and dislocation. These same conditions continue to produce gangs. Today, however, new forces have been added to the equation.

Criminal gangs are changing in ways that were not imagined by most scholars just a few years ago. They are emerging into powerful economic, political and quasi-military forces, with the ability to corrupt judges, police officers, legitimate businesses, family life and schools.

For a long time, people have expressed concern about growing crime and organized crime in North America. Organized crime, as we know it today, had much of its origin in youth gangs and the production and sales of illicit goods (alcohol) during prohibition. But those who are worried about organized crime haven't seen anything yet. Many youth gangs are now rich in money in every sense of the word. They can buy and sell people, and they do.

One frightening omen is that the age range of gang membership is increasing. Traditionally, gang membership began in mid adolescence and continued to early adulthood. We now have illicit gangs with memberships ranging from ages eight or nine to the early forties and numbering into the thousands. Small children identify with and emulate their heroes in these gangs. They assume a quasi membership role in anticipation of the time when they will become full-fledged members. The gangs are becoming tribes in every sense of the word.

Young children are used to distribute drugs and for other illegal activities. This is done to protect the older gang members from facing prosecution. Gangs know that the courts are loath to punish young children for criminal offenses. More importantly, using children provides a tested source of new recruits.

Contrary to popular belief, gang membership is no longer confined to the lower class or to urban minorities. Middle class youth, rural youth, and those of European, Asian, Latin and African ancestry are being associated with more and more illicit gang activity.

Gangs are penetrating more of our schools. While the problem is most visible in large inner city schools, it is by no means limited to them. At the current rate most of our suburban schools will share the experience of gangs. Perhaps, then, appropriate attention will be given to the problem.

The resources of these youth gangs are reflected in their ownership of expensive cars, vans, real estate, communications systems, international connections and large amounts of ready cash. More importantly, these gangs are securing large stockpiles of firearms, including automatic weapons. These weapons are carried not only on the streets, but to school. The school in many areas has become the focal point of drug deals and acts of extreme violence.

Accompanying these frightening weapons is a value system which encourages their use. There seems to be little or no concern for the consequences of using guns to enforce their codes and sell their services. Like political terrorist groups, these gangs have a cult-like attraction. There are many young people who are willing to kill and even to die for their gangs. In several large metropolitan areas, gang related murder is the leading cause of death among young people.

Gangs like the "Al Capones," the "Crips" and the "Bloods" of Los Angeles are spreading from city to city and country to country. In almost every city of any size, connections and supervision by centralized gang forces is occurring. What are the implications of this growth in nationally and internationally organized gangs for our schools? Among them is the inability of schools to protect their students, turf wars, lower educational achievement, high drop out rates and values contrary to decency and good citizenship.

Some educators are aware of these threats posed by youth gangs and they are seeking solutions. School attempts at controlling the problem have included the use of metal detectors, random searches of lockers, security patrols, and vigorous expulsion policies. Some have strictly banned all gang related insignia (e.g., hats, scarves, jackets, graffiti, etc.). These kinds of interdiction in our schools, however, fail to significantly deter the development of gangs. This is because these types of restraints fail to deal with the real dynamics behind gang growth. In fact, if not done carefully, such interdiction can increase the potency of gangs.

Schools are where much of the gang's recruitment, socialization and control takes place. Most urban schools are simply too understaffed to meet the competitive forces that these gangs impose as they imprint their values. Often teachers are willing but they only have time to reach a few of the many alienated students they see in a day. Classes are too large because teachers are too few. The first step, therefore, is to hire more teachers so we can have smaller class sizes.

Yet even with more teachers, there will not be the necessary impact. As a group, teachers must also be given more skills than currently provided by most universities. Those who only intend to teach their traditional subject matter will be of little relevance in reducing the influence of gangs or in being effective instructors of subject content. Teachers must teach their subject matter, but to do so they must know how to reach their students. If they are given the resources to do this, there is hope.

In fact, schools are our only hope. If given the opportunity and resources, we can educate most young people to be resistant to the kinds of values and opportunities that illicitly oriented gangs provide. If we don't improve our schools by reducing class sizes and providing teachers who can do more than merely cope, nothing will work.

The police cannot stop the growth and power of gangs. The police and courts have been beefing up their war on drugs and gangs for years, and yet, drug use and gang activity are increasing. This growth is a fact. We do not mean to say that laws and their enforcement are irrelevant. We only mean that the courts and police cannot do the job alone. Furthermore, our law makers, police and courts can—and often do—make matters worse.

There is a need for a change in our economic and political positions. For instance, one may not feel that the legalization of illicit drugs is the answer. However, one would be mistaken not to recognize the economic power of a system that offers young people thousands of dollars for selling drugs versus a system that offers, at best, minimal wages—even if jobs can be found. Something must be done to stifle the economic attraction that drugs provide. This is not a task for the schools, but the current economics of drugs is a powerful force with which our schools must contend. But even if the economic attraction of drugs is taken away through decriminalization, our schools' task still would be formidable.

There is a principle summarized by Robert K. Merton which helps us understand why so many of our young people are attracted to gangs. When individuals subscribe to the culturally valued goals of money, status and power, and the legitimate means of achieving these desired goals are perceived as blocked, then they will probably choose from among the available illegitimate opportunities (e.g., drug selling). Gangs offer in their recruitment a way for their members to achieve money, social standing and power. In the face of this, what is the school to offer?

Simply put, it is our task to help students find legitimate routes to achieve the goals of pride, productivity and civic responsibility. However, without a change in our educational delivery system, there is no hope that the demand to participate in gang life or the demand for the wares of gangs (i.e., drugs, prostitution, power) will be lessened.

This book by Richard Arthur takes a hard look at the gang problem. As an educator, he brings to bear decades of experience in working with gangs in the Los Angeles and San Francisco areas. He has seen it all. And most of what he has seen applies to every country in the world. Mr. Arthur has had failures in working with gang members. He has had successes.

Much of what Mr. Arthur illustrates is that schools can reduce the attractiveness of gangs. He suggests that the only way for the school to reduce the attractiveness of gangs is through the "bonding" of students to teachers, to classrooms, to school, and to their communities. Mr. Arthur shares with us how this bonding can be produced while preparing students with the knowledge, skills and values for making healthy choices.

Gangs and Schools is his story, but it is also the story of young people caught in the web of gangs. In a forthright manner, Richard Arthur tells us where we have gone wrong. More importantly, he tells us much of what we must do to remedy the problem. Although there is ample reason for despair, the insights of Mr. Arthur give us reason for hope.

Alan McEvoy
Wittenberg University
October 1991

Acknowledgements

Special thanks goes to my former students from the following schools and colleges:

Virgil Junior High, Los Angeles
Washington High, Los Angeles
Jefferson High, Los Angeles
SER, Jobs for Progress, East Los Angeles
Huntington Park Adult School, Los Angeles
Paramount Adult School, Paramount
Cerritos Community College, Norwalk
Chapman College, Orange
California State University, Los Angeles
California State University, Long Beach
Long Beach Community College, Long Beach
Compton Community College, Compton
Merritt Community College, Oakland
Alameda Adult School, Alameda
Castlemont High School, Oakland
Fremont Adult School, Fremont
Newark Adult School, Newark
Logan High School, Union City

A very special thanks to three of my students who are still my best friends: Fernando Gaxiola an Attorney in Tucson, AZ, Sal Rivera, Director of a job training program in East Los Angeles, CA, and Evelio Rojas, an administrator at the Department of Motor Vehicles in Monterey, CA.

My students at Jefferson High School in South Central Los Angeles, provided me with much of the material included and inspired me to write this book.

1
THIRTY-FIVE YEARS OF GANG LIFE

Innocence described me when I began teaching over thirty-five years ago in a junior high school in Los Angeles, California. There were members from three large gangs in my homeroom and they made their presence felt, the least of which by wearing their jackets and insignia. That first year was painful, especially when three of my students were killed. But I did begin to learn how to relate to gang members and how to help many of them who would have otherwise been harmed.

In 1959, I transferred to a large city high school
where there were other gangs, but they were less active and I had a slight respite from gang intrusion
into my classroom.   However, things got worse.
Eventually, turf wars, thievery, drug abuse and intimidation became habitual events as the gangs jock-
eyed for power. For whatever reason, I got involved.

Fortunately for me, my skills in working with
gangs improved. In 1966 I was assigned to work with
several gangs and their members.   Most of these
gang members were dropouts from the regular high
school who were now in a vocational center.

I transferred again to another high school in
1968. Here the gangs were not only active, but there
was a lot of student unrest. My job included going
into the neighborhoods and getting the gang members to go back to school. I seemed to have a great
deal of success. However, we did have a problem in
keeping them in school, most dropped out again.

Three years later I became a principal of a high
school in Northern California where there were
many active gangs. Almost the first thing I did was
to meet with their leaders and ask for a truce on
campus.   Fortunately for me, they agreed.   Our
school became neutral territory. While I was there
we worked closely with the neighborhood churches

to assist them in helping gang members in their parishes and congregations. Unfortunately, both we and our neighborhood clergy suffered many failures. Our students were killing each other on a regular basis. Nonetheless, we were able to help quite a number of them. Some graduated and a few went on to college. However, we always thought that our most important successes were those students who became good citizens regardless of their gang affiliations or how far they proceeded in school.

During this period, we also started a special vocational summer program. Many gang members attended. We used federal funds to pay them for work and we started an alternative street academy near where most of the gang members lived. We rented a store for the academy and we placed several teachers and a counselor there. Student attendance was greatly improved. We had few rules, but those that we had, we enforced. We did lots of interesting things like planting crops in the back of our school and giving the food to our student's families.

In 1975, I started another gang project and it was funded for three years. Many enrolled. This time, the city allowed us the use of a neighborhood recreation center. We offered classes and a sports program. We again used federal funds to provide job training and remedial help for those who needed it.

Several earned school credits and returned to their high school. Some were placed in entry level job positions. Like before, a few went to college. Still, we were never totally pleased with our efforts. This was because several of our students were killed in gang fights and others were convicted of crimes while conducting their gang business.

Then, starting in 1980, I joined a special neighborhood program for young people. In so doing I met with several gang leaders. Again, I made a deal with them. I promised to give their members training and jobs if they would make our schools neutral territory. The arrangement worked better than anyone predicted. The gang members were paid to paint over graffiti throughout our community. Some painted murals. Others cleaned the houses and yards of senior citizens. Some were trained as mechanics or aircraft workers. Others were taught reading and mathematics so that they could earn their diplomas. Again, some went to college. It was a great program but it ended in 1983 when the government terminated funding. That was the year I returned to high school as a teacher. I knew that dangerous and illicit gang activities would increase as the program ended. And they did. The neighborhood is more dangerous now than ever before.

In summary, for over three decades as a neighbor-hood counselor, teacher and principal, I have con-fronted gang problems, worked with gang members, and have had many successes and failures. What have I learned during my long tenure?

I have learned to feel like a war correspondent whose words can never fully describe what I have seen. Nevertheless, I am compelled to write. It is my hope that what I have experienced will help me to help others embattled by gangs. I trust it will help them know that if we use our school resources better and do the right things, we can have hope.

2
THEIR WORLD, OUR WORLD

Three of my students were killed that first year I taught school—thirty some years ago. No, this does not reflect the harsh reality of my experience. Three of my students were executed, assassinated, or murdered. This shouldn't have happened.

They were children growing up in neighborhoods where youth gangs were rampant—where turf wars, trade wars, drugs, homeless children, guns and cynical values prevailed. Their values rejected the dreams of most of us for justice, opportunity and achievement through hard work and education. This depressed me; an innocent first year teacher, from a working class background, who sought the pride of being an effective teacher.

That first year was a cultural shock; and, if it had not been for the goodness and caring of some of my students then, and through all the years of my teaching, I would have given up. I would have become bitter and alienated. I would have seen no hope for stemming the poison that gang life poses, not only for the poor and disenfranchised of the inner cities, but for all of sane society in all of North, America. But I believe—indeed, I know—that it is still possible to turn things around and reduce the spread of gangs. This belief has helped to keep me from giving up.

We must solve the swelling problem of youth gangs, if for no other reason than because it is critical for our own well being. We simply cannot afford the illicit character of these gangs. They must be checked, but I question whether the police, the courts, the jails and the parents of our young are as yet equal to the task.

We cannot expect a mass of children born to children, drug addicts, alcoholics, child abusers or criminals to learn at home the proper values, aspirations and skills for meeting either their needs or society's needs. There are other masses of parents who must live in the war environment of gangs, who do not have the skill to cope for themselves, let alone for their children. Most try but many fail. Yet all their children end up at school; many are "last chance children." If not helped in school, their lives, if they survive at all, are likely to be filled with misery.

Furthermore, even those of us who are able to raise our children to avoid membership in gangs, have little relevance as far as other children joining illicit gangs. We who do well to take care of our own do very little to reduce gang growth. Similarly, those parents who have taught their children to say no to drugs have not stopped the growth in illicit drug use.

Those who may think that the phenomenal growth of illicit gang life in our cities is not relevant to them—perhaps because they live in some well-kept suburban neighborhood or they live far away in the country—are mistaken. The growing youth gangs undergirds much of the drug distribution network for sales to rich and poor alike in every part of society; it portends an organized crime scene we haven't seen the likes of yet.

Where can we as a society turn for help in reducing the existence and impact of youth gangs? There is only one institution left that one can legally orchestrate to deal with this problem—the schools. Yet, as currently structured and staffed, the schools

cannot do very much either. There is hope, however,
if we are willing to make certain changes. That is
what this book is about. But first, consider how
gangs are playing out their existence in our schools,
particularly in the inner cities of urban areas.

GANGBANGERS AND ALIENATION

During one of my early classroom discussions, my
students began talking about gangs and drugs. I
soon realized that I did not understand many of their
words. I wrote a few down and asked them to help
me with the spelling and what they meant. Immedi-
ately my class volunteered to make up a test for me,
which they did. I failed their test. It reminded me of
the Black English test I took years before. I failed
that test too.

Jerry, one of the students who helped make up
the test, said he had been a "gangbanger" (belonged
to a gang) for a long time. He said the gangs got to
him (i.e., made him see the value of belonging). One
day, he said that he almost killed someone from
another gang and was sent to jail. When he got out,
he was a hero, but "things got worse at school." His
school work suffered because he was getting drunk
rather regularly on beer and hard liquor. His time
was also taken up with gang activities and selling
drugs.

Jerry looked out of my classroom window and saw some young men walking by. "Those are gang members," he said. "They like to walk the halls. They don't go to class." I didn't know any of the young men who were walking by, but I had seen them before. I went outside and asked them where they were going, but they kept walking. I asked if they had hall passes. They ignored me and walked faster. They walked right by a school security officer but he didn't stop them. I asked the officer if he recognized the boys. He didn't seem to know what I was talking about.

There wasn't time for me to leave my classroom to be chasing either students or non-students. Jerry had waited for me. He wanted to tell me that he had enjoyed writing the vocabulary test for me to take.

GRAFFITI MARKS THE TERRITORIES

Graffiti, much like the urine of dogs and cats, stakes out territory over which domain is claimed. I have copied gang graffiti from the walls of classrooms, school buildings, bathrooms and neighborhood buildings and fences. The graffiti is often used to show that a particular gang has the right to sell drugs in a certain neighborhood, just like an insurance salesman has his "territory." In the Los An-

I copied the following graffiti from buildings near the school.

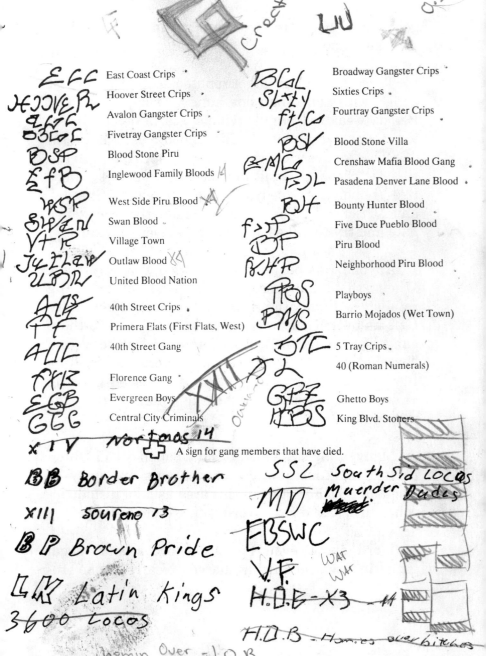

East Coast Crips

Hoover Street Crips

Avalon Gangster Crips

Fivetray Gangster Crips

Blood Stone Piru

Inglewood Family Bloods

West Side Piru Blood

Swan Blood

Village Town

Outlaw Blood

United Blood Nation

40th Street Crips

Primera Flats (First Flats, West)

40th Street Gang

Florence Gang

Evergreen Boys

Central City Criminals

Broadway Gangster Crips

Sixties Crips

Fourtray Gangster Crips

Blood Stone Villa

Crenshaw Mafia Blood Gang

Pasadena Denver Lane Blood

Bounty Hunter Blood

Five Duce Pueblo Blood

Piru Blood

Neighborhood Piru Blood

Playboys

Barrio Mojados (Wet Town)

5 Tray Crips

40 (Roman Numerals)

Ghetto Boys

King Blvd. Stoners

A sign for gang members that have died.

Border Brother

Souseno 13

Brown Pride

Latin Kings

3600 Locos

South Sid Locos

Muerder Dudes

EBSWC

V.F.

H.D.B - X3

WAT WAT

H.D.B - Homies over bitches

Jasmin Over Bitches - J.O.B.

geles area there are two main groups—the "Crips" and the "Bloods."

These two gangs are supposed to be the largest gangs, with more than one hundred subgroups. The Bloods wear red handkerchiefs, scarfs or shoelaces; the Crips wear blue. The Bloods use the term "Crabs" to describe the Crips; the Crips call the Bloods "Slobs." Gang members have street names like "Lonely," "Greedy," "Dog," "Silent," "Speedy" and "Cricket." The students claim the two gangs hate and try to kill each other whenever they can.

Anyone can be jumped by a gang at any time. When that happens, usually the other gang retaliates. Retaliation is usually brutal. Many have Uzis and other automatic weapons. Where do these gangs get their guns? They often receive them from "baseheads" (i.e., drug addicts). Because both the Bloods and the Crips are heavily involved in the drug underworld, it is easy for them to obtain all the guns they want.

Many of my students attend what they call "ditch parties" at houses where the parents are away or working. Such parties in this area usually include alcohol, drugs, and sex. Word gets around quickly.

Word about even more dangerous and illegal gatherings is also quickly shared. Nearly all the students know which houses are "rock houses," (i.e., places where crack cocaine and other drugs are sold). When one rock house is shut down by the police, another one, maybe two, quickly takes its place. The students always seem to know about these new houses, almost before they open for business.

The young people in this area also know that the police are flooding the neighborhoods with over one thousand officers every weekend. They know that the police are out to destroy the local gangs. However, most people in this neighborhood, including those outside of the gangs, believe that all the police in the world cannot stop drugs or gang activities. They know that the drug pushers can be and are very bold. Dealers are arrested, then are back on the street in a few days. And if not, there are several who compete for their places. When particular gang members feel harassed they simply move to other areas. But always, fear, gangs and their products (i.e., drugs, prostitution and intimidation) are nearby and under some gang's jurisdiction and protection.

I asked Jerry, one of my students, what he liked about his gang and he said, "I get protected. What else is there? Before I became a "gangbanger" guys would beat me up and take my lunch. Now my gang protects me. Everyone has gangs. I get respect now. I had more respect in prison than I do now in school."

Another student, Claude, drew a picture to illustrate his belief that our students and our community are surrounded by gangs and that drugs are everywhere; that the politicians, schools, police, mafia and drug sellers, try to keep young people and others who must live in the community poor and ignorant. He said that they want people to be this way so that drugs will continue to be a way of life.

He cited judges, politicians, preachers, police officers, and yes, even educators as "on the take." If Jerry is like lots of other students, I surmised, there is a clear break down in the essential "social contract" of our society. And, as I was to learn "no one trusts anyone" is rapidly becoming a description of the alienation characterizing the people where gangs operate.

Consider, for example, Geraldo. He was a gang member I initially disliked. I probably resented him because he disrupted my class every day. Geraldo swore too much, drank alcohol between classes, practiced extortion and hit young women at school. I visited him where he lived in a third floor apartment. He was babysitting his four younger brothers and sisters. The sink was full of dirty dishes and the younger children were running in and out. He surprised me. He told me—I who disliked him—that I was his favorite teacher. He also said his father had been beating him regularly. In summary, I learned that Geraldo was raised in a home that hated our civilization. So did Geraldo. I attended his funeral.

One day after school I asked Maria why she didn't do her homework. She started to cry. Later, I found out she didn't have a place to sleep that night. She was frightened and bitter. Probably, she wouldn't mind if the rest of society suffered her fate. And, I was to learn, she too was alienated from much of what our society values.

One day I got "on Ramon's case," a senior, because he wasn't turning in his work and was sleeping in class. I learned that he works from 8 p.m. until 3 a.m. as a janitor. He supports his entire family with his earnings. I knew he was a good young man, but I worried that if things did not change he too would become bitter and estranged. He did.

What did I learn from Ramon, Maria, Geraldo, Claude and many others like them? I learned that we adults are often quick to judge these young people. Because we seldom have the time (or inclination) to get to know them, we often fail to see their humanity. Their humanity, however, is surprising given their condition.

Some of my students see drugs being sold every day. Some are gang members who have been wounded or who have served time in jail. Some are on probation. Several have been killed because of drugs. For example, a few blocks from a school I taught in two young women were murdered because they were in a red car and they were mistaken for young women who were supposed to deliver drugs to a rival gang.

Almost any drug can be bought at or near the school. This implicates not only students. Some say they have seen school employees entering rock houses where drugs are sold. One student said she bought drugs from a school employee at the junior high school she attended. Many others claimed to have known teachers who used or sold drugs. Why shouldn't such students feel alienated?

I asked my students what they thought about the "Just Say No" to drugs campaign. They laughed. One student, Billy, said, "It's a big joke." He went on to explain that "the United States paid General Manuel Antonio Noriega of Panama while he was selling drugs." I was surprised that he knew the general's full name—he said his father is a fan of Noriega and refers to Noriega by his full name to show respect. He said that nothing would be done to stop the sale of drugs or the need for drugs.

Another student explained why he likes drugs. Rocky said drugs make him feel good. He said he comes to school high because it's the only way he can put up with his teachers and the "stupid rules." He likes to "trip" and argues that it helps him study and relax. I suggested that he see our school nurse. But if being of help is a criteria, that was poor advice. The next day Rocky was absent and I never saw him again.

DRUGS ARE THEIR BUSINESS

The "high rollers" or big drug sellers operate like entrepreneurs. They share their profits with their helpers, often with those who are much younger, mostly in elementary school. They are called "peewees" or "wannabees."

Parents may help their "peewees" by protecting them from the police. Some cooperate with the drug dealers because they have no other way to buy food or pay their bills. Some are happy to see their children come home with hundreds of dollars. Some are ashamed, but they still take the money.

Some of my students carry a lot of cash. Recently, a former student of mine came in, waved a roll of hundred dollar bills at me and laughed about my being an economically "poor" teacher. Another student asked me if I wanted a piece of the rock. He meant rock cocaine. He called a $25 piece a "dove" and a $50 piece a "bone."

Most of these students did not make good grades in chemistry, but they explained the chemical process involved in using baking soda to cook the cocaine. When it gets hard, it can be sold in small pieces as crack. It seems my students know the manufacturing side of the business quite well. This is sad.

They also claimed that some who sell drugs do not look like drug pushers or members of a gang. Rather, they look like typical middle class students. Because of how they look, no one suspects them. They also might have regular jobs so that no one questions where their money comes from. One student said of a straight "A" student, who he thought looked like a nerd: "He is a big drug seller and an important member of a gang."

Of course, we all know that it is extremely dangerous for anyone to sell drugs if he or she is not affiliated with a gang. The gang does not allow outsiders to sell drugs. There is too much money in drugs to overlook such an intrusion into the territory of their own "high rollers."

Many big rollers often show off by showing themselves "draped down" in gold and expensive jewelry. They drive big, expensive cars, may carry Uzis or other automatic weapons and are usually older than the rest. What makes them most dangerous, however, is that they are often role models. The others look to them for guidance and as economic success stories.

One student and gang member explained his reasoning to me this way: "If I can make up to $1,000 a day selling drugs, why should I work at a job for minimum wage? I'm better off on welfare than working. I want to be a 'high roller.' How stupid do you think we are?"

THE PERVASIVENESS OF GANGS

As an educator with over thirty years of experience in working with gang members, I have seen first hand evidence in Los Angeles, San Francisco, Oakland and elsewhere that these gangs are not unique to particular urban areas. Large cities such as Chicago, Cleveland, New York, Vancouver, Dallas, Milwaukee, Toronto, Atlanta, Miami—the list is too long to mention—have similar problems with gangs, even though not equally publicized. So do smaller cities such as Dayton, Grand Rapids, Akron, Gary, East Palo Alto, Portland, Orlando and elsewhere. Gangs are as pervasive as are the conditions which produce them.

The gang problem is also going to become much worse. Gangs are attracting more and more members, and they are becoming more violent. Drive by shootings, a symptom of gang activity, is getting worse all the time. One reason for this is the unholy alliance between youth gangs and international drug sales.

Even a cursory examination of newspapers from cities throughout the United States and Canada reveals a portrait of communities struggling to fight the use of illicit drugs. Police departments are also noting a rise in gang activity related to drug sales. Further investigation will show that drug sales are, by and large, not the result of independent individuals trying to make a dollar. Rather, organizations are at work.

Youth gangs—even if not seen by the average citizen—are critical for the effective distribution of drugs. Furthermore, huge profits are attracting increasing numbers of vulnerable youth. These youth are grouped into gangs for self protection, monopoly of sales areas, networking to assure drug flow, and money laundering. Even in upper class areas where no gangs seem apparent, if crack or designer drugs are present on any scale it is almost certain that youth gangs are somewhere in the picture. "Turf" battles have been transformed into "trade" battles in every sense of the word, with deadly violence used to secure markets. To be sure, if you have a drug problem, wherever you are, gangs are there too.

3
REASONS AND
CONSEQUENCES

✦ **W**hat is causing so many of our young people in urban areas to join gangs? Obviously, those who are members of gangs anticipate getting something out of their membership, but what? My experience is that many are moved by their desires to overcome the feared experience of personal failure. Others connect with gangs because of intimidation and social pressures. And still others join because they believe that either the legitimate means for achieving status and success through schooling is denied them, or, that not going to school is too costly in terms of economic, mental or social demands. As an educator, it is frustrating to see these conditions causing so

✗ many young people to commit themselves to illicit activity.

What I find equally frustrating is that whatever the reasons for joining a gang (and they vary from case to case), failures in both school and personal life inevitably result in more attachment to gang life. Even students who are high achievers in school, who have high self-esteem and so forth, become "outsiders" with serious personal and social adjustment problems after they become members of gangs.

EVERYBODY LOSES

Consider the story of Lorenz, a gang member I knew for a number of years. Lorenz was born in Spain and moved to the United States to be raised by her aunt after her parents died. Lorenz was ten at the time and well-adjusted for her circumstances. She grew up in a large urban Hispanic barrio in San Francisco.

At first, school was difficult for Lorenz because of her limited English language skills. She had difficulty understanding her teachers and they had difficulty understanding her. They could not speak Spanish. However, one teacher was especially kind and caring and helped her to learn English. She also received help from her English as a Second Language and in the eighth grade, she understood most of her teachers and she was making friends. Lorenz, at this time, seemed to have no more problems at home or elsewhere than do millions of other normal children. Unfortunately, it was then that most of her social and emotional problems began.

Lorenz became involved with a number of students at school who called themselves a gang. They got along well and protected one another from other young people. They ranged in age from thirteen to eighteen years. For entertainment they sometimes got drunk and drove around looking for fights with other gangs. Nonetheless, while problems were emerging at home during this time, at school Lorenz was still doing well and she was pleased with her classes!

Lorenz went on to high school, she liked it at first. She took academic courses and did well. Her social life at school, however, was quite different from her previous year. In high school, unlike her junior high experience, about eighty-five percent of her classmates were black and about twelve percent were Asian. There were only three Hispanic students with whom she identified. Lorenz began to associate more and more with these Hispanic students who were already members of a small gang that resented school. Like them, more and more Lorenz began to skip school.

Lorenz and her three school friends said they didn't like their teachers or the way they were being treated by the other students. For her and her friends, high school was becoming unbearable. Lorenz then did what many students do when they believe their lives are unbearable. She rebelled. She used bad language with her teachers and misbehaved. This resulted in her teachers refusing to intervene on her behalf or otherwise help her. Things got worse and she failed one class after another. Lorenz had become a student with all kinds of difficulties and was seriously "at risk" for even more problems.

In high school, Lorenz also began to believe more and more that she could not learn what was expected of her. She misjudged her teachers, she misjudged what could happen to her, and she misjudged the motives of her aunt and friends. She felt alienated in the sense of feeling powerless to do anything to control her destiny. Lorenz was by then deeply estranged from her school and her aunt. She was almost emotionally "addicted" to the "high" her friends could provide. To add to her problems, Lorenz found escape from her pain and boredom through alcohol. During her first year in high school, Lorenz was almost thoroughly debilitated by her condition. She could only live one day at a time. She was incapable of deferring gratification in order to meet her future needs. What happened next?

In an effort to help, Lorenz was pressured by her aunt and teachers to attend summer school to make up for her academic failures. As luck would have it, she had as her teacher in summer school the very one who had given her failing grades before. Unfortunately, her grades in summer school only got worse, as did her attitude, Lorenz again skipped most of her summer school classes. Usually she went to the beach with her friends. Thus, in the fall Lorenz found herself repeating the same classes. She was ready to drop out of school. For her there was no satisfactory life apart from her friends.

For all of these problems, however, her problems were just beginning. Lorenz and her friends were now into heavy drug and alcohol use. This got them into trouble at school and into even more trouble with the police. One night Lorenz and her friends went "cruising" the streets. She saw a parked police car and, with the encouragement of her friends, decided to cut its brakes. She was caught, arrested and sent to juvenile hall. When she got out, in frustration her aunt (who was also her adoptive mother), severely beat her. She threatened to kick

Lorenz out of the house if she didn't stay away from her gang friends.

Lorenz, however, only pretended to follow her mother's advice. She sneaked out of her home to be with her gang friends, a few of whom were homeless. One gang friend had a job and supported the others. Another gang leader who lived above a garage told Lorenz that she could live there. Lorenz was only fifteen years old.

One day her mother caught her with her gang friends and again beat her. When questioned, all that Lorenz seemed to remember about her life at home during this time was that her mother yelled at her constantly. Lorenz was miserable at home and couldn't stand being there for more than a short time. To further complicate her life, Lorenz continued to drink and use drugs. One result was that a policeman on a motorcycle arrested Lorenz on suspicion of using drugs. Yet the police had to let her go because there wasn't sufficient evidence. Later, when she saw the policeman's motorcycle, she wanted to damage it. She was filled with distrust and hate for authorities.

She then ran away and lived in the garage with her gang. She was there for several months. The eight of them did nearly everything together. They used alcohol and drugs, engaged in sex and endorsed violence. They also had guns. The leader gave Lorenz an automatic weapon which she kept for as long as the gang was her "family."

Yet living in a gang is not easy. Personal conflicts and dissonance are common. Lorenz decided to move from the garage to the streets with other homeless people. Her friends fed her. She found a place to sleep in a park behind some bushes. The police could not find her. She kept drinking every day.

All the while Lorenz was living in the garage and the park, her mother looked for her. Her mother did not know that Lorenz would regularly walk by her house but wouldn't go in. Finally, the police caught Lorenz. They took her home. Lorenz was "near the bottom." She was filthy, distraught, ill and physically exhausted. This time, it appeared Lorenz was ready to change. She said that she sincerely wanted to get along with her mother.

Her mother, however, wouldn't talk with her about anything that seemed personally important. It seemed as if there was no stable, healthy adult with whom Lorenz could communicate. She only felt comfortable talking with her friends. She could talk to them about anything. She believed that her gang

respected her and cared about her. To Lorenz, they
were family. However, her friends didn't come
around for several months. When finally they did,
Lorenz ran away once again to live with her gang on
the streets of San Francisco. Why? Lorenz, had
many things working against her which were not
true when she was twelve, including:

- engaging in extensive substance abuse;

- having a low self-concept of her ability to do
  well in school;

- making low assessments of her value to
  others;

- holding very distorted views of herself and
  others;

- being alienated from school and family; and

- being unable to find gratification except
  through contact with her gang.

Lorenz was now being seen by most of her
teachers as a "loser," an "uncooperative" student
and as a violent gang member. She was now truly an
"outsider." As such, she was looked upon as unwor-

thy of their limited time. Lorenz was in serious
trouble and her life chances were poor, indeed.

Lorenz's case is somewhat typical of many who
join gangs. She was inducted into gang life, not because of a deficiency in her psychological state or bad
relationships at home or school, but simply because
her gang initially offered her opportunities to have
fun, overcome social rejection, experience excitement,
share camaraderie, gain some autonomy from adults,
and otherwise feel good about herself.

These are the kinds of reasons for most people
joining almost any clique or organization, be it Boy
Scouts, churches, sororities, school clubs or other law
abiding groups. The difference for Lorenz is that her
gang approved of and encouraged her in activities
that were counter to the public good, and fostered
values and beliefs which impaired her. This in turn
caused problems at home and with her teachers.

Most people have long known the disastrous effects of the wrong friends. The gangs about which
this book is written are more than "the wrong
friends." Many of the youth gangs operating today
are crime academies in themselves. They teach their
members to value delinquency or crime, to successfully engage in illegal activities such as drug selling,

to avoid being caught, and to manage the organizational and business aspects of illegal conduct.

HITLERS AND THE FEARFUL

Of course, there are young people joining gangs who already hold all the values espoused by gangs. Unlike Lorenz, these persons usually have serious psychological problems at the outset. Those with low self-esteem, those with low self-conceptions of ability to achieve in socially valued settings like the school, those who have intense cravings to escape reality through drugs or fantasy, those with delusions of grandeur, and those who thoroughly hate themselves and legitimate social institutions, are all likely recruits for gangs. In fact, if gangs were not present, those in the inner cities with intense needs for control would probably create gangs. Gangs, for them, are seen as an important source of power.

OTHER FORCES

There are other conditions that increase the attractiveness of gangs. Among them are needs to feel secure, to have trusting relationships, to be valued, and not to be bored. Gangs are often the only family for young inner city youth. Adam, a gang member, said to me when I was inquiring about his younger brother:

"He hangs around with a gang for protection. There is nothing for him to do. There are no recreation programs. The school doesn't like him and won't help him. He's too young to work and too young to drive. He might kill someone someday. Maybe he'll get killed. He's going to hang around all summer with that gang and get into trouble. There may not be one person who cares about him. He doesn't even care about himself."

Adam went on to suggest in various ways that unlike school, the gangs provide young people like his brother with a sense of dignity. He said, "A kid can get to like his school just the way he likes his gang. But his teachers and principal will have to respect him just like the gang respects him. My brother feels good when he is with his gang. My brother feels bad at school. The gang is his family. The gang is where he can talk to someone and be listened to."

Adam then asserted that gangs will always attract students, no matter what the police or other people do. He said:

"In my gang, you are just like a soldier. It's easy for us to recruit future soldiers for our gang. All the kids want to join. They don't like school. We keep hearing about kids that don't learn, but they learn a lot from us; and they learn quickly. We've even taught some of them some math and how to read. Why don't they read in school? Maybe there is something wrong with the school, not us."

Adam paused for a moment, and then continued.

"Are people better just because they are older? I know that some people just look at me, and seeing that I am in a gang, think I'm stupid. How do they know just by looking? I hate it when someone treats me bad just because of the way I look. I know guys that are never bothered by the police or teachers, but they are worse than the guys in my gang. They look straight and no one suspects them. The principal likes them because they look good to him. He doesn't know how really bad they are. The security guard never bothers them like he does us. It's like we have a big sign on us that says "we are bad" yet it's those other guys who are the bad ones. They will really hurt you."

In summary, everything that Lorenz and Adam said typifies the hundreds of young gang members I have known. Regardless of why they joined a gang they came to suffer from:

Cause mentality

- poor self-conceptions of academic ability and self-esteem;

- perceptions that most adults and authorities are uncaring, selfish and dictatorial;

- feelings of powerlessness to achieve a desired life style through education;

- feelings of insecurity regarding their neighborhoods;

- resentful attitudes toward their schools, and even their families;

- a belief that educators are not to be trusted but that their gang would never do anything to harm them; and

- sensations that their gangs are exciting while their schools are boring.

Thousands and perhaps millions of people have had the same miserable feelings and dysfunctional perceptions as did Lorenz, Adam, and his brother, but they did not join gangs. Many older people today had all the same kinds of emotional problems as do adolescents today, but they did not join a gang. Why

didn't they? For most of them the reason is simple.
For most of them, the gangs as they have come to be
were not present in their life when they grew up.

They may have had emotional problems but there
was no gang to recruit them or they saw other
legitimate opportunities for coping. Many of these
legitimate opportunities included work. Today, un-
employment in our inner cities is so great that only a
few can have even the lowest paid jobs. In the past,
even those with little schooling could meet their felt
needs through work; they could find work.

On the other hand, today most everyone wants
cars, fancy clothes and so forth and this takes
money; money which is either legitimately or il-
legitimately acquired. Advertising and the media
have done their job. Now schooling is more critical
than ever, and felt needs demand more schooling or
else the taking of "short cuts." Today, short cuts for
many urban youngsters are their gangs and "doing"
drugs.

It is easy to infer that young people join gangs because they are mentally or emotionally disturbed, are
stupid, or are otherwise "losers." My experience suggests otherwise. What some believe to be the causes
of joining gangs are, more often than not, the outcomes of gang membership.

The example of Lorenz, like so many others, suggests that she was bright and capable before she joined the gang. She was not a "loser." After joining the gang, however, her attitudes and skills deteriorated. And the gang continued to reinforce this deterioration.

Restated, my conclusion is simple. When our young people perceive that there are no available and acceptable means for achieving through schooling the legitimate goals that are promoted in school and the mass media, then the illegitimate means offered by gangs and drugs are likely to be taken.

Restated, most young people who join gangs are often no different than those who do not. It is a mistake to only look for unique psychological drives. Gang members want essentially the same things as do others. They are products of the same forces which shape the needs and aspirations of the rest of us. They want opportunities for respect, acceptance, personal achievement, status, material well-being, autonomy and a sense of having a measure of control over their own destinies.

The critical difference for gang members is that legitimate opportunities to achieve these ends are often—correctly or incorrectly—perceived as blocked. If legitimate opportunities for success in school, social acceptance and meaningful employment are believed by them to be denied, and a gang offers alternative means for their attainment, the path of the gang is likely to be chosen.

As educators, what do these beliefs mean for our reaching out to help these students? We can partially answer this question by first being clear about our goals. Then we need to recognize the importance of certain conditions that will restrict who we can reach and save.

4
REACHING OUT

$\mathbf{E}$very responsible educator seeks to provide those conditions which foster in their students:

- feelings of pride, competency in learning and hope for their futures;

- skills and knowledge in areas that have value to our culture; and

- attitudes that reinforce a democratic society.

There is little argument over these values. The debate begins when one attempts to say what skills and what attitudes are most needed by students. Even here, however, there is some consensus. Nearly every school in North America offers instruction in the "three R's," art, music, physical education, social studies, science and health. The real issues are not so much with our goals, but rather with how we shall achieve them, that is, the quality of education we shall provide.

Here our attention seems to focus most on expenditures that should be provided for education; the content of course offerings which should be offered, and the preparation and conduct of teachers. All of these areas are pertinent in regard to their effects on the relevance of gang life. Is this concern sufficient?

Certainly, unless teachers are knowledgeable about the content they are charged with teaching, then no program for reducing the power of gangs will be very effective. However, that is not by any means, our biggest problem. Most teachers know their subject matter reasonably well.

They also are sufficiently well-trained to enter middle class schools and learn their craft of teaching. What they are not usually prepared to do is to enter a typical inner city public school and be able to reach out and become significant others to street hardened students. What is worse, when they can't, they often think there is no way of reaching these students. But there is.

Fortunately even teachers without proper college training can quickly learn the necessary skills for working in the inner city if they have the proper attitude. Unfortunately, it is common for new teachers without appropriate experience or attitude to be assigned to inner city schools. By the time they have gained sufficient skills, they use their seniority to move to less demanding cultural situations in middle class areas. Those that are not given the opportunity to move to what they consider better schools, often quit, suffer from burnout, or take their frustrations out on their students. If properly selected and given inservice preparation, however, working in an inner city area need not pose a cultural shock for young teachers. Further, if new teachers are not given overcrowded classrooms, receive support from their colleagues and have sufficient teaching resources, they are not likely to want to leave for other schools.

If teachers are forced to teach large classes in the inner city then they will not have the time to meet individual needs. Thereby many programs for reducing gang influence will be seriously impeded. This is a major problem in most inner cities because family support for specific educational instruction is often missing.

In my judgement, family support is usually lacking in our inner cities because: many of the parents
are barely able to survive economically, are under-
educated to meet their children's needs, have more
than their share of heavy alcohol or drug use, are
homeless, are themselves children, or they live in
neighborhoods where crime and powerful gangs rule
the turf.

This means the schools need to be able to do at
least one thing before they can provide a quality
education in poverty areas: reduce class sizes to less
than twenty.   This needs to be done from the
primary grades through high school. And at the earlier levels up through sixth grade there should be a
teacher's aide in the classroom. The importance of
reasonable class sizes and added help for teachers
was recognized in the successful Head Start program. The facts are that if you are going to reach
out to street hardened youth and turn them and our
inner city war zones around it will take one teacher
for every fifteen to twenty students plus one teaching
aide.   Teachers must have the time to work with
every pupil if they are to overcome the typical bur-
dens of inner city life.

Until such time that we reach a consensus on
what should be taught and what children should
learn, the best and quickest way to improve inner

city schools would be to reduce class sizes especially at the elementary school level. As a beginning the approximately one thousand inner city schools in the USA should have reduced real class sizes to no more than 15 per teacher and teacher's aide.

The counselors too must be given the opportunity to use their skills in working with students and parents. Unfortunately, counselors are now being used in many schools for doing mostly administrative chores like scheduling. In most schools they have no time for "real" counseling.

Obviously such educational reforms which call for a considerable increase in expenditures are largely beyond our concern here. Furthermore, I am doubtful that our leaders are ready to give leadership to such major reforms. In the short run, for them, it costs too much money. I believe that in the long run what is happening in our urban schools is going to cost us much more, not only in terms of money lost, but in terms of freedom from violence and a loss of our traditional freedoms.

Civic responsibilities which protect our freedoms cannot be coerced by the police, courts and more jails. They occur only when individuals have the skills, resources and values for participation as "haves" and not as "have nots." What then do our leaders want, what does society really want, and what can we do to lessen the magnitude of gang influence?

Regardless of the quality of the program we offer, we can make matters better or we can make them worse. Our mission as educators is to make matters better, even if in the long run our society fails its young. Of course, our modest mission of doing better rather than worse is not likely to be attained unless we learn certain things about the street life of many inner city students. We need to take advantage of what we know about those who have quit their gangs and turned their lives around to become responsible and achieving students. There are lessons to be learned for every one of us.

5
LESSONS TO BE LEARNED

It is a myth to believe that youth gangs meet all the emotional needs of their members. Typically, gang members go through very dehumanizing hazing as part of their initiation. There are usually fights to determine each one's place in the pecking order and often they are required to make extreme personal sacrifices. In other words, it is not easy being a gang member.

Why, then, do so many stay in gangs? Why don't they quit if the costs to them are so great? Why do gangs seemingly remain so compelling to so many? One answer is that it is often safer to remain in the gang than to drop out. The gang provides protection

from other gangs, from authority and from itself. To
quit may mean to risk reprisal.

Another obvious reason for staying in is that
gangs provide at least the illusion of opportunities
for gaining money, power and status. Very often,
these opportunities are genuine and no illusion.
Even though these opportunities may be illegal,
many see no alternative.

Included in the commitment to gang life are
values which despise the legitimate routes of work
and schooling.   It is these values, along with
demands for compliance to gang rules, which make it
difficult for members to leave. As the gang becomes
"family," rejecting the legitimacy of school, traditional authority, work and community values is ac-
celerated.

A FORMER GANG MEMBER CONFIDES

I asked Rick, whom I trusted and who was no
longer a gang member, why others did not do as he
did—simply leave. I knew he was very perceptive of
events and was quite objective. Rick said:

"During all my gang years, I had little respect
for my teachers or principals. They were

phonies. They didn't care about me or my friends. They would say that they liked us one minute and in the next they treated us like dirt. A teacher might not use the word stupid, but we knew what she meant by how she treated us. I knew they didn't like me. They didn't respect me, so I didn't respect them!

"Some teachers think we respect them just because they are teachers. I don't. I respect those who are real and respect me. I, and most of my friends, can tell a phony teacher right away. We get sick of them. Lots of kids drop out because of them. A lot of us don't go to certain classes. Sometimes, going to school is like watching a bad movie for six periods a day on television. At least when we watch TV we can switch the channel. We can't switch teachers. If possible, we just don't go to certain classes."

I wanted to disagree, but before I could speak he said:

"A lot of teachers are racists, even if they don't know it. A black kid might see only one black teacher while he's going to school. Some white teachers cannot understand us black kids. Some black kids think that all white teachers don't understand them.

"Most principals are more concerned about power than helping kids. We figure they have to act that way. They should have been policemen. They act like judge, jury and everything when it comes to prosecuting us. It is hard to believe them. They run the school like a prison.

"When we like and respect teachers or principals, we believe them. I would probably do anything for a teacher I liked. But I would, if given the chance, make life miserable for any teacher or principal I hated. We used to put graffiti everywhere, except in the one room of the teacher we liked."

Rick paused briefly and then continued.

"Sometimes we do things just because we're bored, even though we really want to learn. We know that every day we are going to do the same thing in that dumb history class with Mr. B____. He's a joke. Some of our parents had him years ago and he hasn't changed. I like history, but I hate his class. It doesn't matter if we ditch. We don't miss anything. I can get an "A" on his tests without going to class. He doesn't care. We all know he doesn't care. We all know the principal doesn't care either or he'd get rid of him. We would learn a lot more and it would be cheaper if you put us in a room with a T.V. set. Teachers are supposed to be underpaid. He's overpaid."

Rick's case illustrates a few of the typically expressed and felt reasons why some people join gangs, but also why they remain. Clearly, **alienation** from classroom life is a big factor and must be overcome.

But other factors also come into play which keep young people in gangs. Gang members, like others, calculate the advantages and costs to themselves from remaining in their gangs. To the extent that their gangs are perceived as providing valued goods, status, power, money and desired relationships, it will be seen as too costly for them to leave. Consider the case of a gang member I will call Bingo.

One day Bingo needed a ride home after school. As I drove, he pointed out a crack house. He said some of his friends were selling drugs. He said he knew all of the places where drugs were being sold.

Because of so many drug related murders and because of the police sweeps, I asked him why so many were willing to risk staying in a gang. In his own way Bingo explained how drugs have become an institution and how drugs are now an important part of his culture. Some of his friends, he said, were completely dependent upon the income from selling drugs.

Bingo also described how many of the drug sellers had lots of girlfriends. Some of the younger dealers, under sixteen, were giving drugs to older women for sexual favors. He said some young gangbangers had lots of money and often had sex with older women as well as young girls, yet they were too young to drive a car. He said that they met their women regularly at a local park. Every time he went to the park he said he saw a different girl pregnant. Some, he said, had already had babies who were born addicted or with AIDS.

I then turned my curiosity to Bingo's feelings toward the police. Bingo claimed that television, the police and school people often do exactly what his gang wants by their attracting attention to them. He told me that his gang didn't have to recruit new members. All they had to do was wait for a newspaper article or television story, and new recruits demanded to join. Even more important to him, the publicity helped to keep the "gangbangers" active and in their gang. He said, "They got to be in our gang if they want excitement."

Surely, gangs satisfy excitement needs which, once met, (to borrow a phrase from T.S. Elliot) "famish the craving." They create a constant need for more excitement even as they satisfy initial needs. The apprehension of giving up the excitement is a compelling reason for staying with a gang. Many believe that there are no other means than their gang for accomplishing the excitement they crave. Unfortunately, they are often right.

Summarizing what gang members say, we may conclude that they seemingly remain within their gangs because of any number of reasons.

- Their gangs provide a measure of protection and security.

- Their gangs reinforce their alienation from school and community mores.

- Their gangs force compliance.

- Their gangs provide opportunities which are lacking elsewhere.

- Their gangs provide excitement.

- Their gangs threaten their members with
  harm should they leave.

- Their gangs receive major media attention
  which glorifies and makes gang life an
  important social event.

Countering these reasons for staying in gangs is a
huge task for educators and their communities. But
the task is not impossible if we look at those who
have left gangs and have learned to value schooling.

WHY SOME QUIT

Quitting is a very "big deal" for any
"gangbanger." It represents a far bigger change than
when they joined. Sometimes it means giving up
friends who may have indicated they are willing to
die or make other dramatic sacrifices for them. What
teacher can be expected to do as much? What friend?

Quitting a gang may also mean placing oneself in
a dangerous position, indeed. One may even be putting one's brother, sister or parent in jeopardy. Most
people do not know what it means to place their lives
and the lives of their loved ones in danger. How can

we expect young people to so endanger themselves
and their loved ones?

Quitting a gang may also mean giving up on
economic opportunities. In our current economic
order we simply do not have enough vacant jobs in
private enterprise to take care of the basic needs of
hundreds of thousands of urban youth who need
work. Also our governments fund only a few work
programs for a small number of young people. We
have said that the gangs offer money. They offer
power. They offer status. They offer excitement.
What can our schools offer? What can our schools do
to reduce the influence of gangs? What have we
learned so far?

I believe that "gangbangers" are most likely to
quit when three prerequisites occur: 1) when their
gangs produce enough undesired frustration and dissonance in them to make them feel miserable; 2)
when their gangs fail to provide for their felt needs;
and 3) when someone external reaches out and
provides them with an alternative means to be a part
of another significant group, to feel safe, to achieve
at something desired and to have status because of
being in the group. The first two prerequisites occur
quite often, but the third only rarely.

Merely to have gang members leave their gangs
because of frustration or unmet needs is not neces-

sarily of benefit to either those who leave or to society. They may merely move to another gang or become social outsiders. The estranged and alienated of our society are not all in gangs. What is needed is for them to become members of a group which inculcates in them:

• a salient and valued identity as a team member,

• a sense of safety,

• a pride in accomplishing something that both the group and society values, and

• an awareness that what has been accomplished will make for a better future, i.e., there is a sense of hope.

This is where we as educators can become relevant if we have the desire, the time and the resources to become significant others; and if we use our abilities as significant others to reduce their alienation from the process of schooling.

This, however, is easier said than done, especially in our inner city poverty areas where important types of family, community and peer support are often lacking. On the other hand, the goals of providing for group identity, safety, pride, and hope are more achievable if schooling is modified to overcome certain inner city forces. Traditional schooling, which may be somewhat appropriate for upper or middle class settings, is almost totally dysfunctional in our inner city schools. The goals for students are the same but how teachers are to reach out to students in inner cities requires a student-teacher and student-student interaction pattern that is not typically present.

Prior research, too common to report here, shows that for achievement motivation, middle and upper class children do not need their teachers as much as do lower class children. This is because for middle and upper class students their parents and peers tend to reinforce the values of achievement through schooling. On the other hand, for a large portion of lower class, inner city children, having a teacher or counselor as a "significant other" is almost critical for success in schooling. Yet, too many inner city children can go through school without having even one teacher or counselor as a "significant other."

6
SIGNIFICANT OTHERS

To be sure, teachers, counselors, principals and other staff members can become "significant others" to even street "hardened" gang members. By "significant other" I mean that they can positively influence their ideas and feelings. Furthermore, they can do this while maintaining the integrity of responsible educators.

Consider again the case of Lorenz. In spite of being a "loser," in trouble with her mother, the police and the school, and despite being seriously impaired by health, attitudes and habits, Lorenz went on to be a "winner." She left her gang because of an educator who became a significant other to her.

"Why Lorenz Quit"

Luckily for Lorenz, and quite by accident after Lorenz had "hit bottom," a person came into her life who asked little in return except the opportunity to be of help. It was a high school counselor who said to Lorenz on the street, that if she liked, she could come back to school and graduate. This counselor gave Lorenz her phone number and told her to call her at anytime of the day or night and they would talk.

Lorenz told me that at first she was embarrassed about telling the counselor her problems, but it seemed like the counselor might understand her situation. In a way, Lorenz was desperate. She took a chance and called her; and to shorten the story, Lorenz reentered her old high school.

Her teachers told me that almost from the beginning her performance improved. Lorenz said she had tried to do better in school because she wanted her new teachers and most of all, her counselor, to like her. She did not like the thought of failing her counselor. Her counselor helped in many ways, including arranging to have tutors help her. Finally, Lorenz passed her algebra class. To Lorenz, the teachers seemed much better than before. In fact she said "some of them really cared . . ." One nice result, she said, was that she didn't have to go to summer school again.

There were stresses, however. Lorenz said that she felt herself pulling away from her gang because they didn't seem to want her to do well in school. She felt that she was being forced to choose between her gang who had meant so much to her and her mother, teachers and counselor. However, because of her increasing involvement at school she saw less and less of her gang. Nonetheless, she remained friendly with them. They let her know that she would always be welcome with them. But they did not coerce her.

Lorenz then transferred to another high school. It was much different but she liked her new school too. She was able to choose more of her own classes and she felt she had more freedom. At her new school there were Filipinos, Samoans, Asians, Hispanics and other ethnic groups. She liked this. In fact, she liked school so much that she got involved in sports and other school activities. After all the years of frustration, school was where Lorenz now wanted to be most.

Were there temptations to be a gang member in her new school? Yes, of course. There were the "Rockers" and the "Stoners." They were large

gangs. And like gangbangers everywhere they
regularly skipped school. Some members would be
absent for many days at a time seeking to find excitement. Lorenz became friendly with two gangbangers
who later died from an overdose of crack. They also
had a new drug called "ice" which they said was easy
to get and the "high" lasted longer than crack or
weed.

Lorenz said she used to enjoy getting high on
drugs and alcohol. Why didn't she drift back into
her old ways? She didn't because she now had the
loving attention of a mentor and role model, her
counselor, the caring help of teachers and the
camaraderie that sports and other school activities
provided.

Equally important, I believe, Lorenz came to see
herself as a member of a class team in each of her
classes. She was even given special recognition by
her classmates and her teachers as a person who
helped her classmates. She had "bonded" to her
classes and her school. She was no longer alienated
from the educational system. She was not in com-
petition with her classmates, she was there to help
them as well as herself.

For example, there was a special program at
school in which Lorenz was a volunteer peer helper.

She shared the troubles that she went through. She showed others the marks she had on her body from fights and from being beaten up. She was recognized as a veteran. By this time she had also cut her hair and wore a lot less make-up. She stopped wearing gang outfits and looked more like a typical young middle-class woman. Lorenz had matured, the other students worked with her and she with them; I was proud of her. I was on her team.

Another Success: Rick

Every story I have about the many young people in my classes who were able to quit their gangs is somewhat similar to that of Lorenz. They all found someone, or someone found them, and that person offered their hand and their concern. Usually, that person was a caring teacher, counselor, coach, or other school person. Then after being reached out to by a caring staff member the "gangbanger" was "integrated" into at least one classroom to become a "team" member. Whenever I asked one who quit why they left their gang, I heard essentially the same story. Rick, an Afro-American teenager who left one of the most violent gangs in the city, said to me: "Mrs. Johnson cared, she really cared. She treated me like a person instead of just another dumb kid."

I responded: "There must have been someone else in your life that cared about you." But he said

"No, she was the only one that cared." I asked him again to try to remember someone else before he met her. "There was no one else," he answered.

He paused for a moment, and exclaimed, "Only Mrs. Johnson treats us like equals. That's how all kids want to be treated. Teachers aren't any better than me. It's funny, the one teacher I liked and respected the most is white, but I've never heard anyone mention her race. I think she's Jewish, but none of us care. We care about her, too. She is real."

We were both quiet for a moment. He then concluded: "I'm happy because I'm going to graduate. It means I've made it. Not many of the kids I started with will graduate. They've dropped out. I still see them on the streets. Some are in my old gang. I quit my gang because of only one teacher, Mrs. Johnson. She really wanted to help me and I couldn't let her down. I think a lot of those who quit school would still be here if they had met someone like her. Maybe they should bomb this school and start all over. It can't be changed. It's never going to change. It's only going to get worse. Man, was I ever lucky to have her for a teacher!"

Rick said over and over again, in many different ways, that he was not only pleased to have a 'good'...teacher but that he was 'proud' to be in her class—that her class worked together. They [the rest of the class], Mrs. Johnson and Rick were a team.

Two general implications follow from the experiences of Rick, Lorenz and the others. First, as teachers in our inner city "war zones" we need to know how to become "significant others" to our students, even if they are "gangbangers." Second, we need to know how to create the sense of team membership in our classes, just as is done in sports.

PREREQUISITES TO INFLUENCE

In summary fashion, stated one way or another, research suggests that the most important factors affecting a teacher's (or anyone else's) ability to change the beliefs and behaviors of his or her students may be grouped under the communication concepts of *expectations, credibility, surveillance,* and *reinforcement.*

Expectations (as Desire and Anticipation)

Almost everyone in education is aware of the power and role of expectations. We have learned, for example, that holding low academic expectations for students increases the tendency for them to achieve at low levels. We also have learned that expecting people to be delinquent increases the probabilites of their being delinquent. Thus, why not simply tell students to do better, that we expect them to achieve at high levels?

However, it is not all that easy to have students achieving at a high level by simply telling them that is your desire. We see students (and others) every day who fail to do what we ask of them. We also see students everyday who behave just counter to what we ask or anticipate. Some do well when we expect them to do poorly, and others do poorly when we expect them to do well. What is happening when students do not behave as desired or anticipated?

One problem, of course, is that we often communicate contradictory messages. It is a truism in education that we need to let students know both what we expect in the sense of desiring something of them, and what we anticipate will happen. If we do not they may give one message more weight than another.

Many inner city students are told that they *should be* better students but that they are too "dumb." We say to students you should learn something while simultaneously telling them that it isn't possible. When we do this we are creating dissonance and alienation; that is, if we are seen as credible. Our communication of expectations to students should be understood to say that we believe they can and should learn.

There is also a problem, I believe, in the literature about which expectations should be emphasized. Too often, too much emphasis is placed on the goal of a particular performance that is desired, rather than on the *ability to learn* to perform. For example, to say to a student "you can't play a piano now but you *can learn* to play one," places the emphasis where it should be. Helping students to learn that they can learn almost anything is more important than learning any single other bit of information or skill. What I mean is that expectations about one's ability to learn *per se* are the most important things that we teachers teach.

It is especially important for inner city teachers to focus on teaching and reinforcing in their students that they can learn. This is because their students are likely to be the recipients of false stereotypes about their learning abilities because of their poverty, race or ethnic status.

But communicating effectively to inner city youth is often complicated because many of the teachers in inner city areas come from backgrounds which hinder their credibility with their students. Many teachers start with a credibility gap that is no fault

of their own but which must be overcome nonetheless.

Credibility

Our general credibility, which is to say the extent
to which we are believed about anything we say, is
governed by numerous conditions. Among these are
four which deserve special consideration. They are
the perceptions of *caring, trust, expertise,* and *shared
belief systems*. These in turn are affected by all sorts
of secondary attributes which should be irrelevant
but aren't. Our skin color, race, ethnic identity, social status, height, weight and numerous other char-
acteristics often determine our credibility. We must
work to overcome them, and equally as important,
we must avoid letting them shape how we respond to
our students and colleagues. Especially important in
working with gangbangers is to avoid the stereotypes
given to them in the media. Most gang members are
more like everyone else in their needs and feelings
than they are different. To miss this point is to
reduce one's credibility with gang members.

Caring: We all recognize that in caring for
someone we tend to increase our influence over that
person. How much "caring," however, is necessary?
Is it enough for a teacher to only care about how well
his or her students perform in class? It all depends.

It depends, for example, on whether the teacher is striving to foster fundamental changes in a student's image of self and the values they attach to education.

A teacher who wishes to change students to see themselves as more intellectually capable or to behave in accord with his or her wishes in contrast to those of the student's friends, must at a minimum, be seen as caring about them, both in and out of school, and both at the present and in the future. If teachers are seen as such caring persons then they are somewhat more likely than otherwise to be viewed as credible in what they have to say to students about their self-images or values.

Reciprocally a teacher's credibility is further enhanced when the students care for him or her. When students feel better that their teacher feels better, and worse when their teacher feels poorly, inside and out of school, the teacher is—all other things being equal—most likely to be believed in what he or she says about the student. Rick illustrated this principle in his expressions of caring for Ms. Johnson.

Trust: Trust is another important factor in becoming a significant other. Successful politicians know this and so do marketing people. Trust is a particularly important factor in the successful conduct of physicians, and so it is with educators.

Physicians who are diagnosing and treating patients know that for them to be trusted with negative information about their patients (drugs, disease, tissue damage, bone malfunctioning, and the like) that their patients must believe that their doctors will not use such information to hurt them. For both the physician and his or her patient, learning about what is wrong with the patient is important for successful treatment.

Can teachers or others be trusted by their students to know what they feel, think or do? If teachers are not seen as trustworthy regardless of the reason, then teachers are not likely to be seen as credible. On the other hand, a teacher's credibility is increased when he or she is viewed as trustworthy; that he or she would do nothing to hurt his or her students. A teacher's credibility is enhanced even greater if he or she is seen as someone who will use negative information about students to help them. The student's best interests are always seen at the heart of a credible teacher's actions.

Unfortunately, many typical activities in a school unintentionally hurt the credibility of teachers. For example, few students feel free to perform poorly on tests because, unlike in a hospital, information from poor performance on tests will be used against them. Testing is seldom used to help students learn what they failed on a test. Rather, our tests usually occur at the end of instruction and are not the means for finding out what needs to be taught. In an inner city where there is a long history of students failing on tests and being penalized for it, it is perfectly understandable that testing is seen as merely another obstacle. But can or should we give up the use of tests? No.

Obviously, teachers will be required to use tests in their classrooms. Teachers, however, can learn to use them in ways that are helpful. In the next chapter I will point out how cooperative learning teaching methods and Montessori methods usually employ testing in a different manner. There testing is done to improve performance.

My point here is merely that testing need not be done in ways to make it more difficult for teachers to be believed in what they say to students. Testing should not cause teachers to be seen as adversaries. But for this to occur testing must be viewed by students as helpful to them.

A similar conclusion is appropriate for what the teacher learns in conversations and while observing students. Recent work in the area of child abuse prevention and identification, make clear that students need to share secrets and feelings but they need to know that the teacher is always to be trusted to try and help students regardless of what they learn. Similarly, a teacher's credibility is increased if he or she is believed to have no intention of using any information to harm any of his or her students' parents or friends.

Shared Values: Communication experts also have recognized that individuals or institutions which are viewed as sharing certain important values with their pupils, gain in relevance and credibility. Catholics, for example, are more likely to believe the Pope than Baptists. Republicans are more likely to believe Republicans, socialists to believe socialists and so forth. What student images of teachers are critical for teacher credibility? As will be seen in the following section on *Staff Guidelines* (which a student prepared) three conditions stand out: *integrity* as model citizens, *fairness*, and *respect* for the student's culture and personal condition.

Even gang members who are committed to illicit and violent lives have no tolerance for hypocritical and elitist teachers. If a teacher lies or commits any kind of fraud he or she quickly loses credibility. In other words, teachers are held to a higher standard by all students, and if they desire credibility they must strive for that standard.

The messages of equal respect must be clear. To hold lower expectations for inner city students is to be viewed as looking at them as less capable and less worthy. Even gang members desire that their teachers not accept bad behavior or poor performance as inevitable. They want help from their teachers not hopelessness. They want their teachers to share with them a respect for the role of educators. Too many inner city youth do not believe that teachers respect themselves as teachers and this hurts their credibility.

Expertise: Any teacher who is viewed by his or her students as understanding the student's condition, as well as being knowledgeable about realistic alternatives has increased credibility. That is, if the teacher is viewed as knowing what he or she is talking about she is most likely to be believed. This seems so obvious that commenting on it seems trivial. However, we as teachers can easily damage our general status as experts—even if we really are knowledgeable—by communicating that which according to student reality testing is wrong.

Teacher Attention (Surveillance)

The one condition that tends to make a significant other particularly relevant is whether that person is seen as being aware of one's performance. For example, if a student believes that his or her

teacher will become aware of whether he or she does
what his or her teacher desires, then the student will
make more of an effort to do what is expected.

Unfortunately, in large classes it is almost impossible to give attention to all those who need us. I
often had more than 40 students per class in an
inner city school. In the inner city, there are likely
to be so many that require our attention that we can
easily feel overwhelmed. We are likely to feel that
we simply do not have the time to try and learn
about what each student feels, thinks and does that
is pertinent to their school performance. And in
most of our communities there is just cause for feeling this way.

Notwithstanding the burden of large classes,
however, there are some things we can do to increase
our awareness of students and their awareness of
this surveillance. Among them are all the ideas
presented or implied in the next section on staff
guidelines. Two other ideas, I believe, also deserve
consideration.

The first is that teacher testing should be conducted more like doctors do—in a clinical setting.
They examine, make a prognosis given certain treatment, then examine again and modify their treatment according to any progress that is made.

Similarly, teachers should be constantly examining, deciding upon what to teach and how to teach based on the examination, providing the learning experience, examining again, and so forth.

Examination of students does not mean formal tests alone. I do mean that assessments are made of students' work and behavior and assessments can and should be done in a variety of ways. Like physicians, we should depend to a considerable extent on what students say they know and can do. Much of a physicians exam involves interview data and not just formal examination.

However, as we noted before, our students will not share with us what they do not know unless they trust us to not use such information to give them low grades. If they trust us they will not fear our formal testing of them. Students experience anxiety when being tested when they cannot trust that the results will help them. The key is trust and trust should be demonstrated.

I have earned student trust, including the trust of gang members by emphasizing the use of my tests, observations and other data gathered in two ways. I use all the information I have to produce progress reports for students that show their growth and not simply report grades. I strive to place the emphasis

on being able to learn and not on some achievement
outcome alone. One seeming result is that my students share with me much more now than when I
used tests in the more traditional way.

I also learned that it is better to examine regularly and review thoroughly what has been observed.
All educators learn the importance of this idea.
Therefore, it is perplexing to know that so many
classes give a few tests and the students' grades are
given strictly for performance on the tests.

Reinforcement

"Reinforcement" for many is kind of a "buzz-
word" for the punishment or rewards one attaches to
the achievement of expectations. Certainly, when a
student believes that he or she will be recognized
and rewarded for carrying out a teacher's expectations, the likelihood of meeting these expectations
are increased. We also know that reward is more effective than punishment.

Why then is punishment the most common
vehicle we use for trying to elicit student confor-
mance to our expectations? It has not worked in
reducing drug use, crime, student violence, or gang
membership. Our emphasis on punishment has not
worked very well, either, in fostering school achievement. We probably depend on punishment because

that is our tradition. But that part of our tradition is no longer valid, if it ever was, for eliciting the growth and good citizenship of our inner city youth. In the schools where I taught, emphasis was on issuing "failure notices" to students at least four times a year. Many of my students were given five "failure notices" from their other teachers. They knew they were failing and they felt that it was useless to try. It was very difficult to keep them from dropping out.

In attending to our young people we need to emphasize the positive in them. I believe if we turn our attention to rewarding young people for what they do right, and ignore when we can what isn't appropriate, we can make far more headway than is now the case. In any event, we will achieve more credibility if we as teachers do as Mrs. Johnson as she emphasized the good in students, even the gangbangers.

I believe that most of the prerequisites for the effective communication of expectations, combined with credibility, high levels of teacher attention and positive reinforcement are clearly recognizable in the guidelines suggested by my "gangbangers" for communicating with them. These guidelines provide a way of fostering in inner city students an appreciation of themselves as students.

STAFF GUIDELINES

I was never trained to deal with gangs as a
teacher or as a principal. I wasn't even taught to
deal with disruptive students. And I never received
any instruction in college about the various ethnic
groups I would be teaching. This caused me such
problems that I would have quit teaching after my
first year if it had not been for Ernestine, a student
of mine. Every teacher, every semester, should know
at least one student like Ernestine. She wasn't
afraid to tell me when I was doing something wrong.

Ernestine (and other students later) taught me
many things. She taught me that neighborhood
gang activity inevitably spills over into the schools
and tragically affects everyone in society. I learned
this again as an administrator who saw first hand
the high economic costs imposed on our schools and
citizens just to repair the damage done to our buildings as a result of gang activity. I lived the impact of
gangs as I sought to control and teach my classes. I
felt the pain of any decent human being as I sensed
the growing alienation of my peers from their students, and their students growing distrust of them.

Ernestine said that gang members usually don't
trust teachers, but that they are still just young
people who will respond to educators and others who

are "real." Ernestine quickly taught me that I would not be an effective teacher until my students, including the gang members, saw me as non-pretentious, caring of them, honest and "in charge."

Ernestine pointed out that the only way to be in charge of a class and receive the cooperation of gang members is to gain their confidence while still acting with integrity and consistency. *She said that no student, not even gang members, wants a teacher to compromise what is right.*

In order for them to see that I was honest and reliable, she encouraged me to see as many students as possible after school and on weekends. In response, I arranged to take a number of them to the beach, on picnics, and to the amusement park. I also started an after school dance program which helped us all to become better acquainted.

Ernestine gave me another bit of valuable advice when she encouraged me to visit the homes of students. Most of the gang members were living in poverty, their families were in a state of disorganization, and all were living in an environment loaded with social ills. These visits made me appreciate them more for even coming to school. My attitude toward them became more positive.

Fortunately, I became a much better teacher. I know this because they would listen to and confide in me. If your students do not listen to you there is little you can do to help them. And if they do not confide their dreams and fears, you really do not know how to reach most of them.

There were several other obvious advantages in meeting with them outside of the classroom. Most importantly, it became easier for me to deal with their stresses in school because I understood their personal problems, including their drug use when it occurred.

I never accepted the wrong that any of the gang members did. Ernestine said I shouldn't and that most gangs would reject me if I did. They did not want me to approve of what they did wrong. But they did want me to understand their motivations and circumstances.

In regard to their misbehavior, it was appropriate for me, from their perspective, to punish them. Yet I also learned that few punishments helped and others made matters worse. For example, Ernestine said that it usually is not a good idea to suspend students for misbehavior. She informed me that some students like to be suspended. She said that such a "punishment" would never work with most gang members. She was right. I needed these students in school if I was to reach them.

I have never forgotten the other things Ernestine and the other students taught me about gangs. Their ideas for dealing with gang members are as valid today as ever. Many of their suggestions make sense with any student, but are especially valuable regarding gang members. To repeat, here is a brief summary of some of their rules which helped me to reach and help many of them.

ERNESTINE'S RULES

- If you want gang members to like you, be "real" with them as you would with anyone. In other words be sincere and honest.

- Show them, as much as possible, that you can be trusted to not make them look foolish or bad to anyone. If they trust you they will like you more.

- Treat gang members attending school fairly, just like anyone else. Do not play favorites.

- Suspend students only as a last resort. Many students, including gang members, like to be suspended. If they are not in school, how can teachers help them?

- Maintain discipline in your class. This is necessary to earn the respect of all students, especially gang members. They want you to be in charge. Enforce your rules and the rules of the school, or don't have them.

- Get to know every gang member as you would every other student, after school, on weekends, and during the summer. Visit their homes and where they work. Try to know their parents and siblings. Take them to interesting events where they will learn something worthwhile.

- When your students are absent let them know that you sincerely missed them. Find a way to call or visit those who are absent too often.

- Show them that you care if they have a family or personal problem that is hurting them in any way.

- Pay special attention to those who do not live at home.

- In every way imaginable, constantly try to
  help them understand that schooling is of
  value to them in terms of their aspirations for
  pride and self-sufficiency. Gang members, like
  others, will work for something they value, if
  they see a way that is not too costly in terms
  of a loss of respect or a loss of friends.

- Try and understand why anyone who is a
  gang member felt the need to join a gang.

- Give every student some personal attention.
  They all need some personal time. Try and
  provide students who need it individual
  instruction. Look for resources in the
  community and school. Helping a student or a
  students's brother find help for their problems
  is a sure way to influence gang members.

7

CLASSROOM CLIMATE: ESPRIT DE CORPS

While suffering displeasure, I recognized early on that there were too few of us to adequately carry out our tasks. My community would not pay for additional teachers. In addition the principal often used teachers to do administrative chores outside the classroom. Such a procedure resulted in raising the class sizes for all of us. There was no provision for assuring that our inner city youth would receive the attention they needed. It was visible that poverty, drug abuse, and crime were getting worse. They are still getting worse. Simultaneously, gang membership in the United States doubled between

1980 and 1990. It is very disheartening, but it may
well continue to grow until the character of life is so
obviously harmed that society feels forced to do what
is right. I wonder how many innocent people will
have to die before that day comes.

Of course, by then the cost of repair will be exor-
bitantly high. If so, our society may select the option
of being like a third world dictatorship: use violence
and economic pressure to keep those of social and
economic poverty at bay. If this should happen a
relatively few will live the illusion of comfortable
lives. Yet coercion seldom diminishes organized
crime or corruption; at best it merely shifts the site
of its expression.

I do not think that dictatorship is likely. But perhaps I believe this because of my dream that someday society will wake up to what must be done. It is
this same sense of hope and faith among many of our
teachers which keeps them trying to do what they
can, in spite of the almost impossible odds produced
by inner city existence.

Teachers know they are out numbered. They do
not believe that they can stem the tide of young
people coalescing into gangs and a criminal life.
Inner city teachers believe, nonetheless, that they
can be of some help to some students, and so they do.

Most of them give their best in spite of stifling bureaucracies and limited community support for their good efforts.

Thus, teachers should not be overly criticized. In a very real sense, they are merely trying to "hold the fort" against almost impossible odds until help arrives. How can they best "hold the fort?" How can they decrease the likelihood of their students joining gangs, or for those who are "gangbangers," how can they be turned around?

The first answer is that we, as teachers, must not allow ourselves to become so disillusioned as to become impotent. We must continue to save as many of our students as we can until society is awakened to the implications of the virulent war zones in our inner cities. We should then take to heart what is known about becoming a *significant other* and Ernestine's rules for relating to students in inner city areas.

Next, we should consider a few guidelines for enhancing the relevance of our classrooms as group forces. Many of these suggestions apply to any classroom, but they are especially appropriate in inner city areas where there is a heavy gang presence.

These guidelines center on building an *esprit de corps* or pride in one's classroom through cooperative activities. Students who experience a pride in being a part of a particular classroom react to an animating group spirit. The classroom, as a group, gains relevance in the shaping of student values. In other words, students perceive encouragement from their peers to be in step with the climate of values characterizing the classroom.

When you have *esprit de corps*—and the group's values are good and the teacher is a significant other who also teaches these same good values—the probabilities of the school achieving it's purposes are greatly enhanced. This was illustrated to me by Mr. Reeder's class.

ESPRIT DE CORPS

Mr. Reeder's Class

In a large inner city high school where I served— a school where our student gang members were doing extensive harm in their neighborhoods, in our school and to themselves—a new vocal teacher, Mr. Reeder, arrived on the scene. A number of our students signed up for his classes, or were assigned to him with absolutely no awareness of what Mr. Reeder was like, or how he would teach.

To put it mildly, many were gang members who, along with most of his other students, initially had poor attitudes about life, including themselves. They had many, many academic, social and family problems. They, in essence, hated school. In fact, I had just arrived on the scene as the new principal to replace the previous principal who had been murdered. During the prior year several teachers had also been severely battered by students. To make matters worse, several students were killed on school grounds. The school was a dangerous place for every student and every teacher. And yes, I can say for a fact, even Mr. Reeder's students hated school.

What happened to the students in Mr. Reeder's class, however, was a dramatic change. The entire class stopped skipping school. They looked different in how they dressed and in the character of their faces. They became caring and responsible; so much so in fact, that we used them as ambassadors for our school in community programs. A pride in themselves emerged that is a highlight in my life. An *esprit de corps* emerged like nothing I had seen before. They felt pride in being in Mr. Reeder's class. To me this was a phenomenal change in outlook among students who were initially alienated from almost everything at school. And, of course, their new outlook was reflected in their new conformity to school norms, as well as in their new assertive citizenship.

What did he do to instill such a desirable change
in his students? How did he create this *esprit de
corps*? I doubt that Mr. Reeder—like any good
parent, good teacher, or anyone else—completely understood all of the critical social and psychological
forces affecting his influence. Yet we all have
answers. When I asked him what he did to foster the
change, he didn't give me a "long winded" reply. He
said, "My students are my friends. I love them [as a
family]. They are a great class."

It is clear that love can be a powerful force, but is
love enough to account for the dramatic changes in
Mr. Reeder's students? Partially yes, but not totally.
There were other forces at work. After all, there are
many parents and teachers who intensely love their
children and students but do not produce the *esprit
de corps* in their families or classes as did Mr.
Reeder.

In response to further questioning Mr. Reeder
said:

"**We** like each other," "**We** want to be the best we
can. And **we** need to support one another...Most of
my students are in poverty, a few have unsupportive
families, some are in gangs, many have had both be-
havioral and academic problems in school since their
elementary days, and a few are still failing in some of

their other classes. Because of this, **we** must work hard **together** to keep up **each other's** self-esteem. **We** tell each other **we are good**...**They** will be my friends forever. **We** want to be the best **group we** can be...Yes, **we** want to be pleased with ourselves."

Mr Reeder also showed them that he wanted every one of them, including himself, to do well outside of class. In so doing, he demonstrated compassion and understanding for any problem at home or in the neighborhood. He helped them to see that what happens inside of their classroom affects what happens outside, and *vice versa*. He taught them that pride in one arena of life should not be destroyed by embarrassing acts in another.

I have heard many gang leaders talk this way, emphasizing the **we** and not the **I**. They talk about how being a gang member affects every part of their life. They tend to show pride in their togetherness— that they depend on each other. That is why gang colors and the sharing of unique graffiti symbols and language are important to them.

Gangs also seem to recognize the achievements of their group more than those of their individual members. When they recognize individual performance, it is most likely to be for something that, in their eyes, helps their gang. Mr. Reeder, in this respect, was similar to such gang leaders. His pride in his class as a group was clearly shared with his students, and he shared his pride from the first day of school— well before his students proved themselves.

How did Mr. Reeder teach? He worked hard to create a **cooperative** classroom. To sound right as an ensemble requires that everyone work together. Everyone knows that a team effort is critical in a choir, even if you have the most talented of musicians. With many students of limited talent, as was true in Mr. Reeder's class, teamwork was even more critical. He taught them that each part, no matter how small, was important and that no one, regardless of talent, would adequately demonstrate their art without the contributions of every other student. As a result, each felt important. Each knew that the gifted performances of the few were a part of the whole; and thereby, each felt somewhat gifted. Each knew that every other student's performance would be judged by how well he or she performed, as minor as the part might be.

How did this happen? Mr. Reeder sought out each student to personally compliment him or her for *trying* to make the group sound great. He centered these compliments on their *trying* and *learning* and not on their accomplishments *per se*. He communicated by word and deed that all of them, regardless of how well they sang when they entered his class, were *learning* to sing better and better.

Further, he constantly let them know that he *expected* them to work at improving. He expected them to improve, not only in his class, but in all of their other classes as well.

I was astonished at how *aware* Mr. Reeder was about what his students were doing in class, in school, and elsewhere. He seemed to have made it a point to know a great deal about them. Yet from what I could tell he never appeared to be intrusive. Perhaps because the students saw him as both caring and non-threatening, they *trusted* him to know when they were in trouble, as well as when they did something that would please him. And as I noted, almost any modest good deed pleased him.

As he was pleased, he complimented. However, he did not seem to compliment achievement *per se*. Rather, his compliments appeared to tell his students that they were "good learners." While the quality of their singing varied considerably, both individually and as a group, he complimented them all for their learning to sing better and better.

By focusing on how each was learning more and more, Mr. Reeder tended to reduce *invidious com-*

parisons in the classroom. He never compared one student's performance with another. Invidious comparisons are less likely when a teacher compliments each slight increase in performance quality, rather then on the greatness of any performance outcome *per se.*

Equally as important, both the talented and the not so talented are likely to feel better when invidious comparisons are avoided. When this happens, appreciation and envy are more likely to be present in the group than is jealousy. Jealousy is a hinderance to credibility. Jealousy can create distorted perceptions and resentment. Mr. Reeder, by avoiding invidious comparisons, thereby did not jeopardize the credibility of his compliments.

Mr. Reeder further enhanced the credibility of his compliments as he taught them a proper basis for *reality testing*. He taught them the criteria by which they could judge for themselves whether their singing was improving. Here he was teaching them the theory and nature of music and not just how to sing better. By so doing, he taught them how to listen to themselves and how to recognize slight improvements.

In this respect, Mr. Reeder was practicing what Maria Montessori noted was so valuable to teaching and learning. The Montessori Method gives considerable attention to students learning to evaluate their own performances. As they listened to their practice sessions and public performances, using the musical knowledge taught by Mr. Reeder, each one recognized that his or her performance was in fact, getting better. Because his compliments were accurate descriptions of changes in his students' performance and the students had learned to recognize these changes as improvement, he was seen as a more credible person.

The experience of being able to have direct evidence of success that justifies the compliments one receives, reinforces behavior far more effectively then either compliments or direct observation alone. Being able to reality test kept Mr. Reeder's compliments from being seen as mere flattery or hyperbole. The students knew that their performances as a group were getting more and more polished, and they enjoyed this. Each one knew that his or her own performance was getting better too.

Thus, the students received a double dose of pride, pride in themselves as individuals and pride in being a member of a group that was doing something important. Thereby their group became an important influence on them.

Their group took on many of the same influential features as do "significant others." Their class became what some may refer to as a *generalized other*. Their group, as a group, became especially relevant for each of them because each was an active member and not just a "bystander" or individual performer. The expectations of the group, as well as the expectations of Mr. Reeder—their significant other—was impacting on their lives. The vocal class, as a group, was giving meaning to each of its members.

This is how most gangs make themselves influential. This is what every successful legitimate group does to produce *esprit de corps*. The successful group gives to its members a valuable social identity and norms to live by, in addition to an opportunity for personal validation.

Unfortunately, some students who achieve well only experience pride in their own personal success, and there are some who only feel pride because of their identification with some group or community. The truly alienated experience no pride at all. They have no positive social or personal identity.

It is also unfortunate that even among those who feel some pride in identifying with a group or community, there are those who only experience this pride as "onlookers." When such is the case, the group has limited influence over them. When one has vicarious identification with a group, then that team has much less relevance to that person than it does for the team's active members.

Knowing this, many groups seek to foster active *participation* among its membership. Being active on a group's behalf tends to *bond* one to the group as a whole, as well as to individuals in the group. Mr. Reeder had his students working together in many more ways than just singing together. They planned and did things together for their community and also they teamed up for nothing more than entertainment. They bonded together as a team.

There are other less important ways by which bonding to a group is encouraged. For example, a bond is often facilitated by giving a group a valued name. Recognizing this, Mr. Reeder did what is characteristic of gangs. Every gang gives itself a name. He gave his vocal class a name. He called them "The Castleers," and he used the name over and over again. Soon no one referred to "Mr. Reeder's class," they referred to "The Castleers" and his students said with pride that they were "Castleers." He had given them a "handle" by which to recognize their new team identity. He gave them a name which helped bond his students to one another. He gave them a name they came to value.

Like the gangs, I believe Mr. Reeder's class gave
his students a type of learning experience—*cooperation*—that was prized. While learning to sing, they
learned much more. They experienced the fun and
value of cooperation. All together, their pride in self
and their pride in their class identity, coupled with
the valued experience of cooperating with others to
achieve what they could never achieve on their own,
proved to be a powerful force in enhancing their
class's influence.

The force of cooperation when it occurs is powerful, indeed; and cooperation can characterize any
group, regardless of whether the group is in a gang, a
chorale, a football team or a classroom. The combined forces of pride in conjunction with cooperation,
produces an allegiance to the group that is summarized in the expression *esprit de corps*. The summary power of *esprit de corps* turned the attitudes
and behavior of Mr. Reeder's students around. I too
received some of my biggest thrills and extra special
feelings whenever I heard the Castleers sing.

It is *esprit de corps* which makes gangs so potent
in our inner cities. Economic, safety, and security
needs are important, but it is the *esprit de corps* that
summarizes the intense bonding of young people to
their gangs. *Esprit de corps* helps explain why gang
members and draftees in the military are often will-

ing to give their lives for their groups. *Esprit de corps* is an appropriate summarizing description of Mr. Reeder's "Castleers."

The Academics and *Esprit de Corps*

One may rightly ask, whether a teacher of social studies, mathematics, or science can be as successful at producing an *esprit de corps* as did Mr. Reeder. Furthermore, how can anyone expect an academic classroom to compete with the attractiveness of a gang in an inner city area? The task may not be easy, but it can be done.

As the examples of Ernestine and Rick illustrate, or the study of youth gangs bears out, gangs do not provide the kinds of security and hope for the future that is preferred by most gang members. Life is dangerous on the streets, even for gang members, and they know it. The gangs tend to focus on the here and now. Little attention is given to the future. Most members of youth gangs see their future adult lives as something they wish would not happen. This felt estrangement from the future can be used to the school's and student's advantage.

Schools, if reasonably conducted, can help give to inner city youth a realistic sense of hope and confidence in their future. This is something which few

inner city youth gangs can do, even if they wanted.
Young people crave the promise of a prideful future,
regardless of whether they sometimes act as if it is
not important. Students in the inner city are aware
that they can not take for granted, like do many of
their middle and upper social status peers, that they
will have decent jobs, security and respect when they
get older.

Like most of us, all young people desire feelings
of pride in what they are today and as well in what
they will become tomorrow. However, since the future appears to inner city youth as one of little
promise, their concern centers on relieving the pains
of the here and now.

When life for them is difficult at school, the
streets offer fear, and home is an insult, it is understandable that drugs and violence directed at others
becomes an analgesic; an aspirin for masking their
situation, but no cure. And when their self-images as
students are that of "academic losers," they build
rationalizations to defend their self esteem. They
defend themselves with the tools they have at hand,
and they exclude from their action much preparation
for their future. Unfortunately, for many inner city
youth the only tools they see at hand for enhancing
their self esteem are the gangs and their ability to
express bravado in a war zone.

It so happens, however, that Mr. Reeder proved that at least his class could overcome gang influence. A rejoinder might be that academics is at a real disadvantage as compared to a music class in creating *esprit de corps*. Mr. Reeder taught vocal music, and of course, we all like music. Furthermore, choirs require team participation. Hence, the argument is that Mr. Reeder's achievement of *esprit de corps* was a much easier task than would be the case for a typical classroom teacher.

It probably is correct to say that in choir or varsity sports it is easier to produce an *esprit de corps* than in an academic classroom. This is particularly true when teachers dominate class time with lectures, students work independently of others, and where students must compete with one another for attention and grades. It also may be easier in music and sports groups if one only accepts into these groups those students who are already relatively talented. Musicians, for example, already know the importance of working together. For them, personal pride may be merely the result of being selected, or the consequence of their past accomplishments. For them the class may have little influence on their self images. Nonetheless, musical groups and sports teams will have an easier time in achieving *esprit de corps* than academic classrooms because cooperation is a requirement for participation, and everyone understands that.

I am sure, however, that nearly everyone has known of coaches or conductors who have had so-called musical ensembles or sports teams where the team concept was minimal at best. That is, the members of their so-called teams seemed to care only about their own individual performances and recognition; they may even have resented the achievements of others on their so-called team. They may have refused to cooperate or make sacrifices for the team's good. On the other hand, there are teams where very talented individuals play minor parts for the sake of the team. They cooperate for the team's good and thereby feel better about themselves.

What is interesting about this, is that where you have a cooperative effort, the performances of all of the individuals, even the minor players, tend to be enhanced. Everyone is better off because of cooperation. There are few coaches and conductors who do not recognize this. However, not all are equally able to elicit a cooperative effort. What are the differences between coaches who foster cooperation and those who do not?

Remember that in Mr. Reeder's case, even though he accepted students with little talent, he reinforced almost any effort, however slight, that contributed to the group's performance. He also complimented any desirable activity of a member he learned about that occurred outside of his classroom. In his classroom, however, his compliments were mostly for learning and the students' contributions to the group. In this way he avoided invidious comparisons. With this approach he reinforced in each student an appreciation for his or her particular contribution to the total effort, as well as an appreciation for the contributions of others.

Surely, Mr. Reeder was a master teacher. He bonded his students, one to another. This, of course, is what an effective and good parent does in building a strong bond within his or her family. The desirable parent strives to avoid pitting one child against another by any sort of invidious comparison. Each is taught that he or she is a valuable member of the family. That was particularly true in Mr. Reeder's class. It also was true in the social studies class of Mrs. Johnson described by Rick in the last chapter.

To repeat, Rick said over and over again, in many different ways, that he was **proud** to be in Mrs. Johnson's social studies class...her class **worked together**..., Mrs. Johnson, the rest of the class, and he [Rick] were a **team**. He said that it was because of Mrs. Johnson's class that he and many other of her students graduated. He was a former gang member who felt sorry for other students who started

school but who did not graduate. He believed they
failed to graduate because they did not have even one
class in school like Mrs. Johnson's class. "Her class
was like a team," he said. She too, gave her students
identities they valued. Like Rick said: They "...
were a team."

There are, of course, many commonly recognized
illustrations where academic subjects have been successfully taught using cooperative teaching methods;
the serendipitous result of which was *esprit de corps*.
The example of *Foxfire* is among the more famous.
The students worked together to produce papers and
books about their community. Their work became
international best selling books and the basis of
films. Surely, almost every effective teacher has successfully employed cooperative projects at one time
or another. However, cooperative teaching methods
have seldom been the primary teaching method of an
inner city school.

COOPERATIVE METHODS
AND GANGS

This is unfortunate because in over five hundred
research studies, cooperative teaching methods were
concluded to have many benefits for inner city situations. "Research on cooperative learning is over-
whelmingly positive, and the cooperative approaches
are appropriate for all curriculum areas. The more

complex the outcomes (higher-order processing of information, problem solving, social skills, and attitudes), the greater the effects." (in Bellanca and Fogarty, 1990).

While the recent refinement of cooperative teaching models, beginning with the well known work of David and Roger Johnson (1979), was motivated in part to reduce conflict among students as they were desegregated by race, ethnicity, or social economic status, other desirable achievement outcomes also were found. The major findings are that as compared to traditional individualistic and competitive teaching models, students who learn in the cooperative model tend to:

- exhibit higher academic achievement;

- develop greater short- and long-term memory and critical thinking skills;

- act with better self-esteem, school liking, and motivation to participate;

- interact more positively with other students; and

- demonstrate higher scholastic aspirations and more pro-social behavior.

It seems reasonable to conclude, therefore, that in the inner city, where we have largely failed our students with our competitive or individualized teaching methods, that cooperative education should be given a chance.

However, cooperative teaching methods—and there are at least five distinct cooperative teaching methods—require considerable teacher skill and preparation. Without such skill and preparation there will be little cooperation among students, and the outcomes may be worse than if not tried at all.

Furthermore, cooperative teaching methods can not be expected to be successful merely by the edict of some high command. The cooperation of a teacher, a student, or anyone else, beyond mere passive cooperation, is as impossible to attain by giving an order as it is to order some one to only think a certain way. How then do you get teachers to cooperate?

The way to get teachers to cooperate to use cooperative teaching methods is to give them the opportunities to learn about and the resources to implement such instruction. The decision must be theirs. I believe that because of the many frustrations that our teachers in the inner cities are experiencing, most would welcome a chance to have the professional responsibility to consider all alternatives, including cooperative learning.

Restated, certainly not the superintendent's office, the principal, nor parents can order a quality education for our students without our teachers' cooperation. The successful use of cooperative teaching methods is unlikely without their support and in which case, we will continue to fail young people in our inner cities. Yet I believe that with the active involvement of teachers using cooperative teaching methods we will give more of our youth a chance to work togather in a way that will cause them to develop healthier values and needed skills. There is hope for changing the character of our classrooms if we give teachers the opportunities and resources they need. If we do, they will induce an *esprit de corps* in their classrooms.

No teacher and no classroom alone, however, can be expected to be totally successful. Each classroom is part of a larger system and like any system, each part impacts on the other parts. Thus, if we seek to have desirable classroom climates we must also create a context within which such classrooms will be fostered. This means we must create healthy *school* climates.

8
THE LEARNING
CLIMATE AND GANGS

I remember the taunts of several of my students who would pull out rolls of currency and ask if I would ever make as much money. When I asked them about it they usually alluded to making this "big money" as the result of taking risks—risks that might get them into "big time" trouble. At first I talked about the threat of jail as I tried to dissuade them from their nefarious activities. However, most of them (many of whom had been in jail or prison) said that "doing time" was not so tough.

I found this talk to be particularly exasperating. I was frustrated that they accepted the risk of getting caught and of being incarcerated. To make matters worse, any worry they had about going to prison was further reduced by their attitudes toward school. They said that school was like a jail, a place to do "good time" or "hard time." And good time to them meant putting in time without hassles until an escape could be achieved.

For them, what made school a "hard time" place was their sensing a distasteful climate of opinion; a climate that rejected their educability and worth as students. Simply put, they saw themselves as "outsiders" in their own schools; and thus, school for them was a "hard time" place.

Others besides students see our inner city schools as hard time places, too. In fact, school is a "hard time" place for a great many inner city teachers and other staff. They see their work lives as something to be endured until they can escape to their homes—which are often at great distances from their schools. They too feel like "outsiders." And to feel like an outsider in one's own school is to experience the very essence of alienation—to feel that one is an alien in one's own house or institution.

Everyday, there occurs a concomitant feeling of alienation among these educators of not being able to help more than a few students. It is not pleasant to be assigned to teach those who wish you were not there, plus feeling that your efforts will prove futile. In other words, many inner city educators suffer several of the same feelings as do many of their students—the feelings of estrangement and futility, coupled with the feelings of being aliens in their own schools.

What is the reason for such a school-wide climate of estrangement and futility among school staff? In spite of well-substantiated research findings, low student performance—when recognized—is commonly blamed on the students' parents, or their race, ethnicity or socio-economic status, and that nothing they can do would ever overcome the backgrounds of their students. The justification given for these mistaken views is usually the spurious statistical association that often appears between student background conditions and the performance levels of schools.

However, we know that simple statistical correlations can be extremely deceiving. Furthermore, the correlations that do appear are modest, indeed. In any event, these correlations fail to suggest what can be done to reduce the climates of alienation among

staff. And alienation among staff is the one thing
that distinguishes high from low performing schools,
and the one thing that makes a difference in the conduct of gangs in schools.

Often to find practical answers for the causes of
events, including high achieving schools, we need to
go beyond the mere use of correlations and ask about
exceptions. For example, our first question might
be: What are public lower class, primarily black
schools, in decaying inner city areas like, when they
are among the highest achieving schools in their
regions?

Numerous research studies since the seventies
have documented the true occurrence of many successful lower class schools. Many of these schools
are in the worst possible inner city poverty areas. In
fact, there are lower class schools—mostly made up
of poor, minority students—which are very high
achieving; higher than many all-white upper class
schools in the suburbs. Why is there this contradic-
tion to popular view?

The answers which are available and documented
by research provide an important insight for reducing the attractions of gangs, as well as for providing
a quality education for all students. These answers,
to a considerable extent, relate to a certain kind of

morale among the school staff. Or rather, how staff morale, or lack of it, is produced.

It is interesting that not all sources of staff morale are equally important in regard to how teachers impact on their students. For example, low morale related to salary is not nearly as important as low morale related to feelings of futility in being able to teach one's students. The emotional and intellectual stance of educators regarding the futility of working with inner city students is the most important morale problem that must be addressed, that is, if we are to successfully deal with gangs.

A profile of findings from studies of high achieving lower class schools shows that when they occur, *nearly all* of the professional staff take a certain stance toward students. This stance even overcomes much, but not all, inadequate prior academic learning, discrimination, and other undesirable social conditions that inner city youth typically experience. This stance is what some researchers refer to as a positive school learning climate (Brookover, et al., 1982; 1987).

A LEARNING CLIMATE*

The following vignettes taken from the investigator notes of Brookover and his associates illustrate attitudes among the staff in both effective and ineffective school learning climates:

We Are All in This Together

> *The George Washington Carver School** is composed predominantly of black, working class children who are achieving well above the state average. On a recent visit, the Carver staff was asked, "How do you account for your success?" Mrs. Johns, an experienced teacher, answered for the staff, "We are all in this together. We have a job to do. If Johnny doesn't learn to read today, we will see to it that he learns to read tomorrow."*

This explanation of their effective program summarizes an effective school learning climate. *It clearly assumes that all students can learn.* The staff has accepted the responsibility for teaching them. No

---

*This section adapted and reprinted by permission of the publisher from Wilber B. Brookover, et al., *Creating Effective Schools*, Learning Publications, Inc.: Holmes Beach, FL, 1982.
**All names are fictitious.

one person is responsible; they are all committed to do the job.

Don't Make Us Look Bad

A black fifth grade teacher, separated from her husband, moved herself and her three children from Louisiana to Illinois. Her job in a black inner city school had gone well. She had called or visited every parent of her students. Eighty percent of the parents responded that she was the first teacher to communicate positively with them. After a time she began hearing subtle hints about being a "do-gooder" and "apple polisher" from her fellow teachers. When these hints became less subtle, she was forced to start having lunch by herself in her room. It was not long before she was told that "the way it is here is not to make waves, keep the kids quiet with busywork, and read your paper while they copy out of the encyclopedia." She continued her remedial reading work, cooperation with parents and high quality teaching. Results began to show, even though most of her students were far below grade level. Remarks about a woman alone with three children being in a precarious situation really shook her up, but she persevered with her teaching efforts. Finally, she was told outright to

*conform or to expect physical consequences
to herself, her family, car, or home. She
returned to Louisiana. The learning
climate of the school remains unchanged
and the achievement level remains extremely low.*

This case history starkly portrays the negative
sanctions and the power of the social group to set
standards and norms for the school. Often, if these
norms are unprofessional, a good teacher must become a social isolate or finally conform to the negative standards.

The Lounge is for Working

A low income, suburban school composed mainly
of Appalachian whites has unusually high achievement; it has an effective learning climate and is a
successful school. Observation of the teachers'
lounge reveals that this particular school does not
have a socially oriented atmosphere among the staff.
Rather the teachers use the lounge as a serious work
place. Conversations revolve around how to help a
student improve his math, how to overcome a problem, or how to implement a new idea successfully.
Students are not put down, compared to siblings, or
"tagged" with a bad image that precedes them to the
next grade. Teachers believe their children can learn
and are quite visibly proud of their achievements.

The students in the school are industrious, eager, well-behaved, and like to read.

This school is another example of the power of the social group to set standards—in this case highly positive ones. This building also illustrates that behavior in the lounge is often reflective of the overall school learning climate. The true feelings and beliefs about the children and the school are allowed to surface in the informal atmosphere among the staff.

The Grass is Greener on the Other Side

An industrial city in Illinois is split by a river. The east side is low income and minority. A large elementary school is overcrowded (the old mansions of the rich are now subdivided into multiple apartments) and has gone from ninety percent white to eighty percent minority in six years. Many members of the staff are older and have experienced the turnover of student population. The school, formerly a model school, is now low achieving. Comments such as "If I had a class like those kids on the west side of town, I'd really teach them," or "I've got the top ability class this year; maybe if I'm lucky I'll have average achievement," and "These kids' parents just don't care about them so how can you expect them to

learn?" are common. The low expectations
of the staff are reflected in the overall
achievement levels.

These four vignettes are extreme but true examples. Not all schools have learning climates as extreme as those reported here. Nonetheless, the learning climate unique to each school does explain much of its achievement level. However, the one common statistic that is especially pertinent is the association between high staff alienation—low staff morale due to feeling incompetent to reach more than a few inner city kids—and inner city schools. What is the reason for this? The learning climate also is extremely relevant for whether a school is at risk regarding illicit gang activity.

WHO SHOULD WE BLAME

Many blame our teachers for the sad state of so many of our inner city schools. But why, I have asked before, should this be? Our teachers have not had a significant voice in the operation of their schools. They have had little choice in their university training and almost none about what they are taught on the job. Only a rare few are allowed to choose their materials. Very little, in fact, has been left to them to decide about the curriculum they are supposed to implement.

The result has been that teachers feel little responsibility for what is offered in the rest of the schools. They feel that they do well to worry about what goes on in their classrooms. This is another instance of teachers being treated as outsiders in their own schools.

On the other hand, every study of teacher attitudes shows that most teachers want to accept such responsibility for the conduct of their schools, particularly if given a reasonable opportunity to be successful. Most teachers want to improve their schools. This is why their professional organizations press for a bigger role in improving education. Inferior schooling makes the lives of teachers miserable too.

In a recent study of public school teachers identified as outstanding teachers, eighty percent said that the public schools need substantial improvement and nearly all of them wanted a leading role to improve the quality of their schools. But so far most of them are being ignored or cooled out with gimmicks by their administrators, their boards of education or legislative fiats. I believe that many feel despair at ever being allowed to turn their schools around. And when it comes to reducing gang membership, they really feel despair.

Our school building administrators also tend to
feel that there is nothing they can do to impede gang
life, let alone produce quality education for nearly all
students. They often believe that they are being
hamstrung by teacher incompetencies, their super-
visors, and the public. For many building administrators, each day is a day for coping with one
pressure after another, not a day for really solving
problems. Thus, they too suffer from despair, especially when their schools are centers of gang activity.
They believe that they have done all that is possible
and they know that what they have done, isn't
enough.

However, given the backgrounds and aspirations
of most school administrators, and the training they
have received, there should be little wonder as to
their feelings of hopelessness at helping to reduce
the number of alienated inner city youth.

What are we left with? The answer is that a
number of inner city schools are in fact inferior and
are being theoretically administered by alienated
principals, who as outsiders themselves, sustain
alienation among their staffs. There is at the source
of this alienation a climate of opinion that the students—except for a few—cannot or do not want to
learn. This is a long way from what should be the

case, as demonstrated by Brookover (1987) and many other investigators.

STAFF MORALE

In previous chapters I noted the obvious importance of teachers becoming significant others and then creating classroom climates which were characterized by an *esprit de corps*. Yet this isn't enough. We also need a school-wide *esprit de corps*. We need a school-wide "team spirit" of expectations to use a sports phrase because a few good teachers, counselors or administrators are not enough.

Almost every low achieving school will have one or more excellent teachers with great classrooms, but they often function in a sea of despair. The students in a good class cannot be inoculated from the pressure exerted by a sea of alienation. Thus, one of our tasks is to help the entire staff of a school overcome any feelings of despair—or feelings that it is futile to try and teach all students. The principal is the person most responsible for establishing a "team spirit" for the entire school.

The entire staff must be helped to realistically hold three critical views: (1) that they are competent enough to teach nearly every student the knowledge, skills and values required for relatively

high levels of performance; (2) that they can teach
their students to believe that they can and should
perform at high levels; and (3) that as teachers they
will be rewarded for producing improvements in the
achievements of their students, both individually and
collectively as a staff.

As part of this effort we must help those staff
members who lack in skills to hone their competencies. This means that a strong staff development
program must be in place along with a situation that
fosters high staff morale—particularly in regard to
teaching abilities.

What Can We Do?

Changing Staff Attitudes. Of course, telling
educators or anyone else what administrators, counselors or teachers are supposed to be like, won't
produce positive results. To tell them what they
should believe and have them accept our views will
depend on many things including our credibility. If a
large number of educators have been taught to
believe that lower class people are not educable, or
that young people join gangs because they are basi-
cally evil, you have a far different situation than if
they have learned otherwise.

Unfortunately, views about the limited
educability of minority and poor people are deeply

rooted in our economic, political, religious, and social
institutions, and thereby in many of us. These views
of educators about the educability of students are not
easily changed.

Yet people do change in their views toward themselves and their worlds—sometimes for the better.
Thankfully, we know how to increase the likelihood
of desirable views and competencies of educators in
inner city schools who devalue the competencies of
many of their students? That is the gist of such activities as are provided in *Creating Effective Schools*
(Brookover, et al., 1984).

Remove Impediments. Another thing we must
do is to remove as soon as possible any major impediments to teachers being able to teach. As long as
there is a valid reason for their not being able to
teach, mistaken myths about students will be extremely hard to change. For example, when you
have a gang infested school, plus a school where
many students and staff see their school as a place
for doing "hard time," one place to begin is by giving
the staff a chance to do their jobs.

Just as in special education, where we have
learned that most teachers can't be very effective
with large classes of physically, mentally or emotionally impaired students, the class sizes in inner city
schools must be low. We must allow teachers the

time to spend personal time with every one of their students, including those with severe problems of alienation. In the beginning, inner city classrooms will require much smaller class sizes than schools in other neighborhoods. They also will need more counselors, more teacher-aides and more school-home liaison workers. The classes need to be more like Head Start classes where you have one teacher and one aide for fifteen students.

When the school climate has been changed then staff ratios may be increased to be more like those of other high achieving schools. But in the beginning, when alienation characterizes much of life for inner city youngsters the class sizes should be limited to fifteen students, especially through grade ten. Then, the learning climate of the school can be changed to deal with problems like gang pressures.

9
SAFETY FIRST
AND GANGS

Feeling safe in a classroom—in the halls, the cafeteria, on the grounds at school events, and even in the neighborhood—is an absolute must. Everyone should understand that fear and anxiety provide a fertile ground for gangs to exercise their influence. Yet *how* we go about providing safe schools is equally important.

The basic way that schools in the past have fostered feelings of safety has been through the willingness of youngsters and their parents to value the authority of teachers and other school staff. The

staff could then use threats of punishment to keep
order, and such threats created no great revulsion on
the part of students. Do such threats of punishment
work as well today as in the past? Yes and no.

It is my impression, that except where corporal
punishment is forbidden, such punishment is used as
much today as it was forty years ago. And where corporal punishment is allowed, it too is used no less.
Yet our dependence on punishment to control students has, for the most part, failed to keep order in
many of our inner city schools; at least to the point
where the students are sufficiently safe from gangs.
Many of our inner city schools are not safe. The students and staff are vulnerable to violence and they
know it.

One response to this failure—punish students
even more and kick more students out of school—is
perplexing. One should know that such punishment,
in the context of inner city problems and social
norms, won't work.

Yet order we must have, if we are to reach out
and help those we are chartered to serve. Perhaps
this is why so many of us educators now want the
police to do our job—keep order in school.

The Police. The police—sometimes referred to as "resource officers"—have become a part of the regular school staff in both our inner city and suburban schools, both in uniform and in plain clothes. They may penetrate student groups to catch drug sellers, patrol school grounds, monitor students at events and in the halls, and intercede in fighting. Similarly, they attempt to reduce vandalism and other types of disorder. On occasion, they act as educators and teach about drug abuse or crime. In our inner cities, they may also attempt to reduce gang influence by both pursuasion and threat. The cumulative result is that the police officer role in a public school has become a whole new expanded career line of work.

Yet we have seen nearly every such effort to use resource officers fail, at least as far as returning inner city schools to the safe havens they once were. Let's face it, the desperate use of the police to take care of our social ills has not and will not work. The police know this. We have to raise our youth properly for the police to be effective. The police, as valuable as they are, can be little more than a "band-aid," on a broken leg; that is, unless our parents and educators do their jobs well. Nevertheless, we continue to put our emphasis on "band-aid" approaches, while cutting back on meeting educational needs. Given such a situation, there is little wonder that the gangs are growing more potent.

The same failure holds true for using police in the community to break-up gangs. We have seen costly police "sweeps" of anyone thought to be a gang member—where the police picked up hundreds and hundreds of gang members and bystanders in a few short hours, and still the gangs grew in number. Unfortunately, the way some of these police sweeps were conducted they probably caused many young people to join a gang.

Nonetheless, the police must be present in our neighborhoods and schools during these times of crisis; and yes, the police often do provide for a certain measure of safety. They are needed. However, we need to socialize and educate our youth better if we are ever going to solve the growing problem of youth gangs, crime and drug abuse. The police tell us this, as do our clergy, sociologists, criminalists and common sense.

Then why do so many people mistakenly believe that our police and courts can solve the problem of violence in our schools? We recently doubled and then tripled the amount we have spent on law enforcement and jails—and we seem ready to spend even more—all while increasing class sizes. We have reduced the number of educators we need in classrooms to do their important task; the job of instilling skills and values in students so that we may have a conscientious and productive citizenry. In not meeting the needs of inner city students we are making our schools into something other than places of learning.

It is now commonplace for the schools in many inner city areas to be more like fortresses than schools. Some are as hard to get into as any security conscious airport loading areas. Bags are checked, metal detectors are used, and the police scrutinize.

Yet nothing has stopped the ever growing presence of dangerous gangs going into these schools with guns, knives, and drugs. They come to school as individual students, but they act collectively as gang members; and then they act to recruit others to their mentality.

Consider a school in California where resource officers were present. As reported in the *Wall Street Journal* (April 23, 1991), even a school which the reporter thought was doing somewhat well at reducing gang activity was described as follows:

"One typical week this school year in Compton included six arrests, five burglaries, four violent assaults, one knife fight, an extortion, the confiscation of a .25-caliber automatic pistol, one strongarm robbery and one assault with

*a deadly scholastic weapon: A Centennial stu-
dent answered gang threats by smashing a
trophy against a Piru's (a gang member's) head
in the assistant principal's office.*

*"School police officers sit in daily on the
briefings of Compton's regular police to learn
about gang-related incidents outside the
schools. Sometimes, using the information,
Compton school officials have even called gang
members at home and 'suggested' they stay
away from school for a day or more."*

Perhaps this is why some inner city administrators feel so hopeless that they believe they
must have a baseball bat, or the police, to control
their students. A baseball bat, however, in the hands
of a principal for purposes other than that of
baseball or dependence on the police, is merely
another sign of the degradation of our schools and
society. Such administrators have given in to their
feelings of futility. We need resource officers, but
how should these officers serve?

We do not need officers in school who, themselves, display the kinds of "macho" image that gang
members already value. For example, in the *Wall
Street Journal* previously cited (April 23, 1991), a

resource officer is alleged to have beaten up on a student to force him to remove gang graffiti.

"A Dominguez student who identifies himself only as Richard says he refused when Mr. V (an officer) ordered him to erase the graffiti of his gang from a table he had scrawled it on. When Richard accused Mr. V. of hiding behind his badge and gun, the officer, who is average in height, muscular and in his mid-30s, offered to settle the matter man to man. 'I got my ass beat,' says Richard. The graffiti disappeared."

Yes, the graffiti disappeared but the officer was also teaching by his actions that power and violence are acceptable ways of resolving conflicts. What the officer did was criminal; in fact, it was more so than was the writing of graffiti on a table. In contrast to such macho—assault and battery—behavior as alleged above, the officer should have behaved in a professional manner. There is no need to break the law in order to uphold the law.

It should go without saying that school resource officers should be "models," of good citizenship, intelligence, judgement, compassion and of sufficient mental health to deal with frustration. When they fail to conduct themselves professionally their impact can be quite damaging to all of us, including to the credibility of the police themselves. Police brutality with young people is the surest way to produce a brutal society.

Bad Seeds. Another mistaken way to control a school is to exclude all students who don't "shape up." We already have nearly four out of ten inner city youth leaving school for a life on the streets. Furthermore, most alienated youth are not discernably deviant to the point where they can be excluded on a constitutional basis.

And certainly this is true for many gang members. The fact is that a large number of students who are members of gangs—some of whom are among the meanest—are not recognizable by outsiders as "gangbangers." They minimally follow rules of dress and deportment, but they don't learn and value what they should. And even when they are kicked out of school, do they really leave? The answer, as anyone who has worked in an inner city school knows, is that they hang around and still infest other students. In fact, some of the people, who have considerable influence over students in school are not students, they are "kick-outs" or "dropouts."

The truth is that tough, strict school administrators do nothing to educate the mass of students in need, unless they also reduce alienation

among both their students and staff. Even with
more and more tightly run schools, we see the costs
of crime, drugs, welfare, and corruption within our
valued institutions going up. Even with nearly
700,000 U.S. citizens now in jail, corruption and
crime are going up. The U.S. puts proportionately
more people in prison than any other civilized
society—South Africa and the Soviet Union follow—
and still its high crime rate is getting higher.

When are we going to wake up? Students who are
"kicked out" and students who drop out have a
strong chance of ending up in jail. Today one in four
inner city black young men have been in jail, are in
jail, have been on probation, or are on probation.
The statistics for Hispanic and white students who
are excluded isn't much better. By kicking so-called
"bad seeds" out of our schools our society, including
our inner city schools is not getting safer; rather it is
getting more dangerous.

Nonetheless, there are students who must be excluded from school. As Carl Taylor, author of
Dangerous Society, a book based on his five-year research study of youth gangs, notes:

> *I hate to admit it but some of these young*
> *guys are so far gone that they need to be*

*removed and isolated [because they kill so easi-
ly]. They don't know right from wrong...*

Source: *Christian Science Monitor*,
January 18, 1991

There is absolutely no doubt, that some young
people have been pushed "over the edge," and it does
not make any difference why. Teachers in regular
classrooms cannot be expected to teach these
youngsters. On the other hand, they must not be ignored. Special programs must be developed for them
in the community.   However, only a relatively few
young people fit this category. Most are alienated to
be sure, but they can be reached in school and in the
community if a proper hand is extended to them. To
again quote Mr. Taylor, when he points out that we
must not reject these people:

*"Now everybody is going to have to confront
and embrace this kid.   Everybody is saying,
'No, no, no,' to this kid; and who says yes? The
drug guy. He comes in and gives the kid an
apple. The kid bites the apple, and the drug
guy says, 'You're with me.' And then the kid
has money, and he wreaks revenge on all the institutions that said no to him."*

Source: *Christian Science Monitor*,
January 18, 1991

Dress Codes. Along with dependence on the police and excluding so-called "bad seeds," many schools continue to over-emphasize the relevance of dress codes as a way 'of reducing gang influence. This too, doesn't work all that well. Students are clever enough to get around even the requirement of uniforms.

The school may ban jackets of a certain sort, and so forth but if gang members want to communicate their identity, they do so in subtle and changing ways. I have known teachers who were oblivious to the presence of active and dangerous gang members. Everyone else knew who the gang members were.

Why then is there this misplaced attention on how students dress. There is, of course, considerable political or public relations profit in focusing on what students wear. This is particularly true when a population is steeped in myth about clothing and behavior. However, there is little advantage to such naive concern if you wish to reduce gang influence.

The simple fact is that even if everyone wore the same uniform to school the gangs would still be active? Some prisons, where all the inmates wear a uniform, are terrorized by rival gangs, and so are some schools, even though they have strict dress codes.

One the other hand, reducing alienation and improving the values of inner city students will result in more students dressing "better," but turning it around, changing how they dress is unlikely to have an impact on their fundamental values. There are too many well-dressed crooks to believe otherwise.

At times my office staff would react whenever gang members walked in with their bandanas or head bands pushing their hair back. I took one of the gang members to court and I told him to dress up in a suit. He didn't look like the same person with his hair cut and his polished shoes. It gave me an idea. I asked several gang members to dress up in suits and ties. They walked into my office and they were not recognized. The clerical staff treated them with respect and commented on what good looking young men they were. The gang members had not changed but the clerical staff now treated them with the courtesy they deserved.

The lesson is clear, not any kind of dress should be allowed, yet whatever criteria is set should reflect a concern for the income and opportunities of the student, and perhaps for what the general community will tolerate. We simply need to be prudent and reasonable; and refrain from spending too much of our time and energy on what students wear, and more on what students learn.

WHAT SHOULD WE DO?

First of all, it is true that using the police, enforcing school rules, excluding certain deviant students, and having prudent dress codes may be helpful in creating a "surface" kind of order in an otherwise chaotic school. However, at worst, they cause more crime and disruption than they stop. Thus, it behooves us to be careful about what and how we do anything to reduce gang influence.

Yet being careful does not mean that we should be hesitant about dealing with gangs in a direct way. If a school, for whatever reason, is a dangerous place where gang fights and other violence is occuring we must take immediate steps.

An immediate *armistice* is a place to begin. Until other solutions can be devised, an armistice among the gangs is almost the only thing a school can hope for in many inner city areas.

For example, it is critical at the time of this writing to have an armistice in areas like Long Beach, California where it has been reported in the national media that students are now having drills, just as they have fire drills, to learn what to do if they or their teachers hear gun shots. They are taught to drop to the floor and seek cover. Isn't it dreadful

that some of our schools have come to having "gun
shot" drills to attain some superficial sense of safety?

What do these drills do for the learning environment of a school? They breed fear, the very climate
upon which gangs feed. This, in turn, produces more
gun shots. I think sometimes that we are "killing
our patients with the medicine we use." We need
other approaches which will end the violence.

Consider, for example, what a principal in Compton, California recently did to reduce gang violence
in his school. This principal in a city—where not
one block in its 10-square miles is territory un-
claimed by the city's 40 Afro-American and Hispanic
gangs—was reported in the *Wall Street Journal*
(April 23, 1991) as getting results.

The article reported an incidence where the principal observed that a few freshman were taunting
and beating up on an upper classman who was a big,
strong athlete. The athlete did not dare fight back to
protect himself even though he could have easily
defended himself. This was because the freshmen
were members of the *Fruit Town Pirus*, a gang with
the reputation of being revengeful; and their revenge
could be fatal.

The principal instead of calling the police, called the former leaders of the *Fruit Town Pirus*, a gang whose members had been alleged to have been active in crack cocaine trafficking, murders and drive-by shootings. He asked for their help. The freshmen, who aspired to be Pirus street gang members were told by the gang's founders to stop the harassment and go to class. According to the article "Close to a learning meltdown not long ago, Compton has made educational progress. It has done so by learning how to deal with gangs."

There are, of course, several ways of dealing with gangs and the task is somewhat more difficult when two or more gangs are competing for power in the same neighborhood. Nonetheless, principals who work with one or several rival gang leaders, will usually have success as long as they show that the gang's members will be treated fairly.

Educators working with gangs need not sacrifice their integrity either. Most gang members, in fact, appreciate it when the school staff does not condone violence, vandalism or weapons in school.

When I first met with gang leaders I found it rather peculiar that they expected so much of me, the other teachers and principals. Children who would readily steal, who could even kill, did not want hypocrites for teachers or principals; they wanted them to be saints.

Thankfully, however, one does not have to be a saint to make a positive impact on gang members. By merely being somewhat decent and caring there are several steps a school's staff can take to make the security climate of a school a safer one. They can do this by gaining the cooperation of the gangs as well as the other students. Many steps, however, will need to be taken if their support is to be given.

Steps to Consider

Any suggestion for which steps an inner city school staff might take to turn an unsafe campus around, while still reaching all students, deserves a preface about meeting with gang members.

Meeting with gang leaders is required but that will not be enough. What will make a difference in reducing gang fostered violence will be the *principal's attitude* toward his or her students and the street people in the neighborhood. The principal sets the tone for the entire school, students and staff included.

With that said, consider what worked for my staff
in a high school where several students were killed
on campus during the previous year. Fighting at
school was common. Teachers were assaulted. Even
the school superintendent was killed. Many students
carried weapons. The school was simply not a safe
place.

We had to worry about how to stop the killings at
school, as well as to reducing the every day violence
of beatings, intimidating threats and vandalism. We
were charged with doing this at the same time we
were to conduct a school program.

We approached our challenge by deciding to
forego, for the time being at least, the calling in of
the troops "so to speak," and of expelling large numbers of students. We could have done that, but for
some reason we wanted to try other things. We organized our brainstorming and activities around the
following ideas:

- knowing our students and their gangs

- making contact

- meeting with gang leaders

- formalizing an agreement

- providing job placement assistance

- developing a community advisory group

- fostering a church-school liaison

- offering special classes to students in need

- having a breakfast program

- soliciting added incentives for student growth

- teaching respect for rules

- becoming valued as educators

- reinforcing academic expectations

Knowing the Territory. The first step, after meeting and discussing alternatives with my staff, was to find out about the leaders of the various gangs. I already knew which gangs were active, their numbers, and their racial and ethnic make-ups. I also knew about their enemies, as well as more minor information, like their colors, signs, and so forth. Almost as important as anything, I learned about the activities they favored. How did I learn all of this in a short time? We simply talked to students, their parents, the police and our building staff. We quickly put together a description of each gang.

Making Contact. The next step was to determine how to reach the gang leaders. It was quite important that I reach them in a way that would facilitate their cooperation. I did not send messages to them. Rather, I contacted each one personally and invited them to come to a joint meeting with me and the other gang leaders.

I said that I was going to ask them about what they thought needed improving, and if they had any recommendations on how to make our school a better place. I asked that we meet in my office. I had heard that they preferred meeting with other gang members on neutral territory. My office was the neutral site for this first meeting.

Meeting with Gang Leaders. After personally thanking each one for attending our meeting, I next said to them, "What bothers you about what is going on in school and in the neighborhood? What needs improving?" They wasted no time in telling me. Quickly the two overriding concerns became apparent:

- being safe in school while receiving respect; and

- the need to find work and help for their families and each other.

Of course, these gang leaders had their personal ambitions as well. Some wanted to become or remain major economic players on the drug scene, some were concerned about the power they wielded, and some acted like they would leave their gangs if there were better opportunities. Yet for all their idiosyncrasies, they all preferred a more safe "turf," along with simple respect.

Making a Contract. Our first opportunity for achieving a safer school was right there in the room. It was made clear by their expressions of concern, and by my summary of what they had said, that they could determine to a large extent how safe our school was going to be. On their initiative, we labored over a pact which stated what their gangs should and should not do at school. We all signed the agreement—an agreement which made our school campus a neutral territory. I too, for the staff, agreed to do certain things.

They agreed that there were to be no gang activities, weapons, fights or drugs on campus. Furthermore, each gang leader would, without forsaking any honor, tell me if the pact were broken. It was an honorable event for the gang leaders to hold this summit in my office and they treated our pact with respect for as long as I remained at that school. Of course we met often after that first meeting.

On reflection, we had many interesting meetings. At first I was apprehensive about what their responses would be, particularly because I intended to be explicit about what I had no intention of condoning. I would not accept weapons or drugs on campus, and I would not accept any form of violence, or any other illegal behavior. They preferred this, partly because they wanted the school to be neutral territory, and partly because they wanted me, their principal, to be that kind of person.

I believe that with each meeting we became more aware and accepting of each other. One gang leader even brought a "peace pipe" to a meeting. He was dressed in an Indian outfit. I don't smoke, but I held the pipe in my hand, and then passed it around. It was a solemn as well as a happy time. We all enjoyed that day. We had an agreement and they kept their word.

Job Placement Assistance. Perhaps the real reason we were successful was because we did not stop with the agreement. We, the school staff, kept our word that we would do what we could to assist gang members and all other students with finding jobs. We called and visited, for hours on end, with local business people, social agencies, and governmental officials. We found work or job training opportunities for many of our students, and we did not discriminate against the gangs.

This created good feelings because we went to great effort to be fair to all students, including gang members. The fact that we failed to get jobs for but a small portion of those in need did not hurt us. Our efforts were appreciated.

A Community Advisory Group. During this period we also established a community advisory group to help with keeping our students in school. Gang members, as well as other students, were welcomed into this group. They offered several easily achievable suggestions for providing incentives to students to stay in school. This group with gang members on task forces, played a major role in fostering community-wide support for our schools. (This is discussed in detail in the next chapter.)

Special Classes. Simultaneously, while seeking jobs for our students and setting up the community advisory group, we began special classes for students in need of help with English. They knew that for some of them, their lack of English skills would impede them in getting and holding jobs, as well as it was hurting them in their classes at school.

A Breakfast Program. We also established in response to the requests of the gang leaders a free breakfast program similar to that conducted in Head Start programs, and one conducted by the Black Panthers. Of course, this program could not have been accomplished without the aid of the district office and governmental food programs. Within a month of our first meeting we had our own free breakfast every morning before school began.

Teaching Respect for Rules. It is absurd to think that people should have a respect for the law without having been taught to feel good about being lawful. How does one learn to feel good about being lawful? One certainly doesn't acquire this value by watching teachers or resource officers break rules. Those of us in positions of authority, therefore, have a special obligation to be decent, fair and rule-abiding. When a politician, a judge, a police officer, a principal, to name a few, commits a misdeed it should be more despicable than when an average person commits the same crime. We have a right to hold people accountable for the positions we grant them in this world. It is extremely important, therefore, that we educators conduct ourselves in ways that model respect for the rights and obligations of students, staff, parents and every other person. As such, we must never "blink" at illegal or unethical behavior.

We must insist that we conduct ourselves with honor. Our word must mean something. In regard to students, they should be shown wide latitude to allow for their exuberance, but honor among them should be insisted upon.

Fortunately, if there is one concept to which we could appeal to gang members, it is their honor. Honor is already a driving force with them, but it is usually limited to their gang and family. Our tact was to appeal to being seen as honorable by the other gangs, the balance of students and the school staff. We talked about honor in every subtle way we could, in every informal interaction we had with them. We employed the notion of honor because we knew that just'having students follow the rules in our presence was not enough to teach them to value and use those rules when we were not there.

This is especially true if others are allowed to break them or they are applied in a discriminating way. Consider, for example, a case where my Vice Principal and I saw a police officer chasing a student on campus with his gun out.

My Vice Principal ran after the police officer and confronted him. He then requested and then took the gun from the officer inside the classroom where the student had run.

I was extremely upset and insisted that no officer should draw a gun unless it was for his or her protection. I was sure that regardless of whether he was breaking police department rules or the law, it was wrong. The officer then admitted that it was a case of mistaken identity, he had chased the wrong person. That officer could have killed someone.

And if we had not confronted that officer we could have set our mission back on its heels. We might have had more gang violence and resultant killings. Every student knew that that officer was wrong.

After that day I noticed a sharp change in student attitudes. Not only the gang member students, but the other students seemed to have more faith in us. They knew that we expected everyone—students, police officers and staff—to behave in accordance with the rules. On our part, we could not afford to be seen as hypocrites if we were going to influence our students to not only abide by rules, but to value them.

Other less dramatic attempts to develop respect for the law among our students included our insistance that whenever a student was arrested on campus that the principal's office was informed. I often went to the police station at the time of an arrest, to the Court for a hearing or trial, or with a student to a probabtion officer. We were quite sure that in so doing we helped insure, on occasion, that our students' civil rights were protected. At the same time, it gave us a chance to spend quality time trying to effect changes in their attitudes and to talk about what "rights" means, and then about what "obligations" mean.

We also talked about the importance of "due process" in a democracy. Young people in the inner city are constantly in situations where "due process" during arrest and court proceedings is meaningful to them. Either they, or someone they know is caught up in the legal system. Yet seldom does anyone—not even at school—spend time to make clear what "due process" means, or its value.

We began by showing the importance for a gang of having proper "due process" within it to solve conflicts between members. They related to this. We then expanded its application to the community and then the society at large. Finally, we talked about "due process" in school.

Becoming "Coin of the Realm." As educators sometimes we forget that some of our influence is dependent upon being of value to our students in their dealings with others. That we are to be valued in the same way as is money. To achieve a recognition of this value we wrote recommendations to probation officers, potential employers and others for them. These recommendations were based on their behavior at school. It was also worthwhile to write unsolicited commendations to their parents and to anyone else that we knew would be appreciated by the student. Our point was that we wanted to share our knowledge of their good work at school with anyone. We said to them that their good work and behavior at school counted for something.

Reinforcing Achievement Expectations. Expecting students to do well in school has, in recent years, been widely recognized for its motivating power in getting students to achieve at higher levels. But less recognized is that expecting students to do well is not very influential unless two other external conditions are also present: the conditions of surveillance by someone they value and reinforcement for carrying out the expectations.

From the very first "intelligence gathering" period, I asked for and received regular informal briefings from the gang leader's teachers and other

staff on how each gang leader was performing and
what seemed to motivate him or her. This gave me
two opportunities: one, to monitor and reward the
gang leaders with a pleasant comment, a smile, a
thanks for doing something positive, a free ticket to
a conference or whatever, and two, to monitor and
reward in the same way, the staff member for helping the student to make this progress. In the beginning I looked hard to find any slight progress worthy
of praise. In the end, both the staff and the students
were keeping me busy praising them in appropriate
ways.

A Payoff

I'll never forget an incident at Castlemont High.
There was a great deal of tension when Dr. Marcus
Foster, our popular superintendent, was murdered
by a group of alienated people. My staff prepared for
a possible problem. Gang members told me that
there might be a rumble or walkout. I placed staff
members at key doors and areas. I took the door
leading into the main building. The door led to an
area in the center of the school across from the
cafeteria.

Students were being asked by their peers to
"walk out" to protest the killing. Some were saying
things like "Let's get whitey." Some of our teachers
who had been hurt in a riot the previous year were

frightened. I knew our school could not stand another riot, but what could I do?

The students stormed out of the cafeteria and headed my way. I stood in front of the door, alone. Before I could say anything a large gang leader stepped in front of me and said:

"*You all back off now. Ya hear me. Back off. Go finish your lunch. No one goes beyond this line.*"

He tapped his foot on the ground and everyone turned around and left the area.

I must say that I have never been more relieved. The students could have easily knocked me over. Later, when I had a chance, I thanked him for helping me. Perhaps he came to my aid because I had helped him to improve his English. Whatever the reason, he not only did me a big favor, he saved our students from themselves. Later when he had further earned the academic right, others obtained a scholarship for him.

Yet not all persons will have an interest in reducing inner city warfare; and thus my story ends on a sad note. One week after the near riot situation, I was driving near the school. Suddenly, I heard a

shot and and a bullet went through the right front
window of my station wagon and hit the front seat
next to me. Most of the students knew what happened. The gang leaders assured me that the shot
was not gang related. It could have been a sniper.
Nevertheless, I decided to resign and leave the area.
I mailed my resignation that day.

10
A COMMUNITY SCHOOL: NOT A SCHOOL IN A COMMUNITY

In a glib sense I have said that there is no great secret about how to reduce the impact of gangs on students' lives. All we need is to increase the quality of the neighborhoods and schools in the toughest of all settings—the inner cities. Our task is not easy.

Our task is doubly difficult because increasing the ability of schools to service their inner city cummunities cannot occur in the same way as in middle or upper class schools. The needs of the people who are living or working in inner cities are extremely

different from those living without the presence of
gangs, drugs, crime, poverty, homelessness, and community-wide despair. The despair is becoming so intense in many inner city areas where gangs flourish
that the school's ability to function in a decent
fashion is deteriorating to the point of absurdity.

The inner city schools cannot wait for society to
turn their neighborhoods around. Each inner city
school must restructure and expand the services it
provides its neighborhood, and for this it will need
both community and school support.

Some would argue, however, that our schools do
not have the resources for providing anything other
than the traditional school fare. Further, they assert
that the spending of time or money on anything
other than academics is a poor investment; an investment which would yield little in return to children,
schools, or society.

Head Start, however, has amply demonstrated
that schools in poverty areas, by assisting in the distribution of welfare services, can enhance the effectiveness of their teaching. By only one thing
alone—providing good breakfasts—they increased
the learning of vast numbers of young students. A
healthy breakfast turned out to be a good investment
in both an economic and an academic sense. And

Head Start, by providing breakfast and other minimal welfare services, plus its main fare—early education and not merely child care—is but one example of the good that has been done for society by taking a broad perspective of what the schools can and should do for children. There are other "welfare" investments which the society can make through its schools. Some of these investments would be of even more benefit than Head Start—and interestingly, they wouldn't be nearly as expensive.

There will be those, of course, who will still contend that any "welfare" business is the task of our churches, or of our political, welfare or economic systems. They will say that welfare is their responsibility alone.

On the other hand, with the demise of much of traditional family life in depressed inner city areas, the flight of churches to the suburbs, and the loss of job opportunities as businesses have sought safer settings, a growing vacuum has occurred. The only institution we have left to teach millions of young people in our inner cities to be contributing members of society is our school system. Education is the only institution left. As they are currently operated, however, most inner city schools are not up to the task. Yet they can be if their purposes are broadened and certain changes are made.

Nonetheless, it is clear that our schools cannot do everything for everyone. They can, however, do more than what they are doing. Furthermore, they can do it differently and more effectively.

What I am pleading for in the way of funds is relatively little at first so that the economic, social, educational and political benefits can be assessed and community support enhanced. The schools need only conduct a few inexpensive activities to be much more effective than is now the case.

With reasonable prudence our school systems can, in fact, save the taxpayers money and do something which is even more important. They can achieve the school's overriding purpose: that of educating a much greater portion of our young people in a way that decreases their motivation toward crime, drugs or gangs. More of our students will learn to carry out the responsibilities required of a productive and democratic society. Much of this can be accomplished by having neighborhood schools become truly *community schools*.

By expanding certain of the community service functions of inner city schools, if done properly, there will be an appreciable increase in the ability of teachers to reach out and teach those who are currently "outsiders"—including hard core gang members. There also will be an appreciable increase in the efficiencies and input of our other community agencies. For too long our schools and other community agencies have not functioned together as teams. They have acted more like competitors than partners.

COMMUNITY INPUT

Under present depressed inner city conditions, starting a neighborhood program which will have impact on the students must of necessity, directly involve the neighborhood for extensive volunteer input and work. This includes not only parents, but people of all positions, including gang members, who live in the neighborhood. These participants from the neighborhood must be helped to be aggressively cooperative, because any program to be successful must elicit more than passive acceptance, it must elicit real input and active support.

In this regard, one must not forget to elicit the contributions of the clergy and agency workers, as well as law enforcement, business, and political leaders. In addition, I believe that many of our social agencies should be partially integrated into the school. And, the more decayed the neighborhood—in either an economic, social or moral sense—the more that street people and other outsiders must be brought into the school for their involvement.

To do this requires the establishment of a bonding. There must be a *bond* created between most of
the people in the neighborhood and their local
school. Again, the key concept is "alienation." A
bond between the residents and their schools has
long since lapsed in most inner city areas.

Since a large portion of inner city youth and
adults are extremely alienated from their schools,
however, achieving this bond will be impossible; that
is, unless we take certain steps to create a felt symbiotic *dependency relationship*. Symbiotic dependency, a reciprocal psychological and social
dependency, is a key process.

Social or psychological dependency tends to bond
individuals to individuals, and individuals to groups.
Fortunately, we do not have to "reinvent the wheel"
to know the kinds of steps we should take to bond
more neighborhood people to their schools, and in
turn, schools to their communities. Common sense,
common experience and considerable research offers
several ways of "dependency bonding."

A school can achieve this bonding by heightening
in a large portion of its public any one of five important feelings:

- feelings that without the school they would not have, or would not get something they want and need;

- feelings of *worthiness* in helping the school to meet the needs of a group that provides their identity;

- feelings of *competency* in being able to do much more than previously thought possible to make a positive difference in other people's lives;

- feelings that others value *them* for their service; or

- feelings that they *own* their school.

In other words, our schools must foster those feelings which are important for all healthy relationships. These feelings must be fostered by schools among people in their neighborhoods and among the students and staff in their buildings.

Coupled with the creation of these feelings, the community must see their school staff as holding certain attributes. They must be viewed as people who are to be trusted, who share certain critical values, who exhibit the attributes of caring and giving per-

sons, and who are organized to work for that
community's best interest.

If an inner city school is to be viewed these ways
there is only one way it can be organized. *It must be
organized as a true community school, and not merely as a school in a community.* In the latter case, the
school is really an outsider. It is a shame that so
many youth, their parents, and others in inner city
neighborhoods see their schools as merely schools in
their neighborhoods. They do not have a feeling of
ownership.

How does a school become a *community school*—
a school *of and for* all the community—especially
when it would be impossible, or terribly inefficient
for educators to provide many of the services the
community needs? How can our schools do any more
than what they are now doing when their budgets
are limited in resources? How, indeed, can our
school districts pay for more programs? How can
our schools suffer even more disruption in their
management than that to which they are currently
being subjected?

Thankfully, there are some partial solutions to
these problems. Yet the task of becoming a true
community school can only be accomplished if a large
portion of the neighborhood is clearly involved in one

way or another; and it has the active support of the larger school district and all relevant political and social institutions.

To accomplish this task in a neighborhood which is alienated from its school, an approach is required that rarely is needed in suburban areas. Restated, the school must be seen as being a place where *important survival needs* can be satisfied. Next, the inner city school must be seen by the neighborhood as a *source of personal and social identity*, a place where their need to be valued by others can be partially met. And not the least, the school should be seen as a *place of enjoyment and something that is owned by the neighborhoord.*

Our task, however, need not be overwhelming, if we keep as our targets: 1) the bringing of as many adults and youth in the community to the school, as often as possible, to have fun, to serve others, and to obtain assistance with their survival needs; and 2) to place all of our students—not just some—in their neighborhoods to be of service to their community. This should be part of their regular schooling. To ask all of our students to spend a certain amount of their time as students—not volunteers—serving their community bestows respect upon them. It recognizes their worth. Equally important, students serving their community is sound pedigogy.

When community service is properly structured, students can learn almost any academic or cultural expectation held for them in the classroom. Students can learn more effectively by and through serving. Fortunately, I haven't seen more than a few students who didn't love being involved in community service in the 30 plus years I have worked with inner city students.

What I suggest for consideration are three kinds of school-community service programs, each of which are related to one of three primary sources of sponsorship: 1) sponsorship by public and private community organizations including even churches and temples, 2) co-sponsorship by a neighborhood school civic group, and 3) sponsorship by the school district and the neighborhood school. In the latter case, students and certain school staff would be working in their school's neighborhood.

These programs will involve very little in new expenditures. They will, however, involve a slight redirection of currently expended resources and the mobilization of many neighborhood volunteers, students and staff. These programs should foster volunteers from the neighborhoods in far greater numbers than do most outreach programs. These programs will find far greater acceptance among school staff than many other proposed "reforms." This is because educators will have key roles and their professional and personal lives will be made more pleasant.

Restated, with the local school staff providing motivational and consultive direction as well as work, the programs should be co-sponsored by:

• the community institutions serving the area,

• a neighborhood community-school action committee, and

• the central school district as representative of the larger community.

Each of the following are merely suggestions to consider. None of the ideas are original, but seldom have they been given their due at one time since the days of the one-room, rural country school.

AGENCY CO-SPONSORSHIP

Information Services

Often various economic, health, educational, welfare, and recreational agencies and programs, which are supposed to serve inner city residents, are located miles from the people they are intended to serve. As a consequence, many are not served. What

is needed is a local site, but many agencies are too
small to be broken into satellite neighborhood units
with the attendent high costs. Yet a local site is
needed for the dispensing of information and the
provision of screening services.

The local school is a logical site for many community-wide agencies and institutions to issue information about their programs, along with instructions
for initial contacts with their organizations.

A very large number of inner city residents—
maybe most—need information on social security,
child care, health care, employment opportunities,
taxes, food stamps, job training, scholarships,
transportation, GED preparation, adult education,
child abuse referral, family and legal services, and so
forth. If there was someone in each inner city school
who would gladly help them find out what they
needed to know, where they should go, or who they
should see, many would be extremely grateful. They
would appreciate both the school and the community
organizations for offering this service. The school
would be serving a dependency need. The public
image of both the school and the agencies they repre-
sent would be enhanced.

The agencies who participate would also benefit
in their ability to deliver services. Much of the time

of the professional staff in service organizations is wasted by having too many individuals arriving at their doors who are unprepared to benefit from their first visit. Anger, and frustration on both sides results when people waste their time. This would be reduced if briefings were easily available to people before they made trips to agencies.

Because of the cost savings to the agencies, and the small cost of implementation, funding might be sought from a local foundation or perhaps from a "United Way" type of organization. All that would be needed would be funding to rent a small amount of space in each inner city school. The only paid staff needed would be one part-time person hired from the neighborhood to coordinate and assist the volunteers. Volunteers from the neighborhood should be used for most of the staffing. This too would bond more people to their local school.

My experience is that if approached in the right way there are many people in our inner cities, as well as anywhere else, who would gladly give of their time to be trained, and to work part-time in such information centers on school grounds. By working as volunteers in a valued program, and by being continually rewarded by praise from the participating organizations and the school staff, the volunteers would value themselves and schools. This would also enhance the image of the participating agencies. The volunteers, of course, would be major ambassadors back to their neighborhood.

The volunteers, of course, should be trained by staff from the agencies, as well as by the part-time paid coordinator. They should be trained as to any handout materials and verbal information to be provided, as well as to their ethical responsibilities. Most agencies already have brochures and other materials to hand out so this will not add any significant cost to them. In fact, it should reduce their costs.

One might raise the question of whether playing such an informational dispensing role is appropriate for a school. Of course it is. Providing information is what schools are about. It is their reason for being as much as anything else. And if in dispensing valid information to the community, in turn increases a school's effectiveness in dispensing information to its students and inculcating in them decent values, so much the better.

Health Services

One of the major health problems today according to the Center for Disease Control, is the large number of children without vacinations for measles and polio. This is but one reason that down the hall in every neighborhood school building, or somewhere on campus, there should be public health resources. Nurses should not only provide health services to students, they should provide education to parents and others, both individually and in classes. This should be done from the time school opens until six or seven in the evening. That is, a school in every inner city neighborhood should be a setting for public health nurses and other health educators to practice preventive medicine. This service should not only be for students, but for all children and adults in the community.

This public health service could function as a referral source for both public and private health care systems. If more people in our neighborhoods knew they could get on the "right track" to receiving needed medical care at their local school, the school would gain considerably in their eyes as an attractive, trustworthy and expert institution. They would feel dependent on both the health educators and the schools which house them.

Other Agency Sponsored Activities at School

Only two kinds of agency-sponsored programs have been mentioned. Certainly, there are other services which may be offered at school such as a reading or film festival sponsored by the public library, extension classes to provide for felt community needs sponsored by a college, a youth drama program sponsored by a local "little theater" group, a "boys" or "girls" club swimming actitity, and so forth. All of these kinds of programs will assist in bonding people to their schools.

My point is to illustrate that many agency activities can be provided in a school setting which are not expensive and which will benefit both the participating agencies and the school. Such programs will do much to increase the credibility of the school. They will *bond* people to their schools, and schools and agencies to one another.

CIVIC CO-SPONSORSHIP*

With school support, there are many other programs which are appropriate for the citizens to plan and manage. Some can have a vital impact on the education of students, as well as on the rest of the people in the community.

For example, a committee or subcommittee of parents, former students, retired persons, un-

---

*Recently site-based management plans have been given a large amount of attention. These are, of course, community co-sponsorship programs which establish school boards. How to best structure these local boards is yet to be worked out. In any event, what is suggested here is in addition to any site-based or district administered school plan.

employed people, or whomever might set up programs for tutoring, or for providing child care services for teenage students, or for child care for neighborhood parents while they attend sessions at school. They might initiate and staff athletic or dance activities, or neighborhood and school clean-up programs, summer gardens, monitor parking lots, plan street fairs, and so forth.

Sometimes we forget the long term and important effects on social health of joint effort. Successfully achieved joint volunteer effort also tends to be quite entertaining for the participants. And entertainment that would be acquired in a school activity would be a new experience for many inner city residents.

Objectives

One objective should be to have as many different persons as possible involved in planning and operating neighborhood sponsored programs. *Another objective is that whenever possible, these programs should be of simultaneous benefit to the school staff, students and neighborhood people.*

In this regard, the school staff, the students and neighborhood committee may wish to draw up a list of things which each can do to help the other in a personal way which is congenial with good ethics; not just in the classroom but during after-school hours and on weekends. Many teachers, for example, would gladly give up a few hours of their time to assist in teaching or counseling neighborhood parents how to do something or other, if reciprocally people in the neighborhood helped them at their home or at school. If teachers and other staff are treated as members of the community a long step will have been taken in the move to create a community school.

Perhaps, just as in a well run church, there should be a committee to call on school and neighborhood persons who are in the hospital or otherwise in serious trouble. This committee could bring the plight of anyone in need to the attention of school or community persons who could and would help. The need is to foster a sense of *community*. This can be done by keeping the focus on meeting mutual survival needs, serving others, and providing pleasure to one another.

Within the district's budget, the neighborhood through its community-school action committee should be able to decide on which programs (not required by legislative act or district needs) it will sponsor and the neighborhood resources they will allocate to them. If the community wishes to spend its volunteer time, for example, on additional before and after school child care programs, instead of helping in a pregnancy prevention health care clinic, or in a tutoring program, that should be their choice. If this is done a sense of ownership will be created.

Committee Formation

The Steering Committee. Initially, a relatively small steering committee, no larger than nine, should be formed, first by the principal with the advice of neighborhood group leaders who are already committed to school projects. For example, the presidents of the parent-teacher organization, student band parents, athletic boosters, and so forth should be invited to make suggestions. Student leaders, including gang leaders, also should be solicited for their ideas. Turning then to the community, the principal should invite all local political, religious, business and labor leaders to a joint conference for their thoughts and endorsement. In the end, the principal should invite no more than nine persons to be members of the steering committee.

Task Forces. Several task forces should then be established by the steering committee to focus on various areas of concern to the conference. For example, a committee might be set up to consider ways the neighborhood could sponsor entertainment events, another to study ways to help students, another to help youngsters find part-time work and

so on. These committees should allow for a large
number of local citizens to play important volunteer
roles.

The Principal

Initially, the principal should set up the steering
committee but then turn over all responsibilities to
the committee that are not required by law to rest
with the school district. Of course, he should be a
member of that committee.

Why should the principal initially play such an
important role in initially establishing the steering
committee membership? The principal—hopefully
proficient in group processes; a person who would
know how to motivate and facilitate a group so that
it works as a team and not as a vehicle for one or
another *prima donna* or vested interest group. The
principal also would be likely to identify those who
would work. After the initial invitations, the neighborhood steering committee should recruit its sub-
sequent membership. In the initial stages, whatever
the case, the principal should be the one to initially
extend invitations to membership, attempting to include those who already have influence in the neighborhood. This means that gang leaders should not
be left out of consideration.

Gang Members

However, while gang members should be invited, they should not be invited as representatives of their gangs, but as individual citizens of the neighborhood. As they participate they should then be honored along with the others for accepting their school ownership responsibilities. It is extremely important that this opportunity to involve gang leaders and members not be overlooked because they, regardless of one's wishes, shape the values and the behavior of a large portion of their community.

DISTRICT SPONSORSHIP

Community Service

It has been increasingly recognized by researchers and educators that young people in both rich and poor schools are becoming increasingly alienated from society. As Nathan and Kielsmeier (1991) have observed:

"Though [young people] may be in high demand for entry-level employment at fast food restaurants and all-night gas stations, many young people are alienated from the society. They are heavy users of drugs and alcohol, they consistently maintain the lowest voting rate of

any age group, and the teen pregnancy rate has been described as epidemic.

"We believe that these problems stem in part from the way adults treat young people. Unlike earlier generations, which viewed young people, as active, productive, and needed members of the household and community, adults today tend to treat them as objects, as problems, or as the recipients (not the deliverers) of services. Young people are treated as objects when they are routinely classified as a separate group; isolated in age-based institutions, and beset on all sides by advertising. . . . they are treated as problems when they are feared, criticized, and made the focus of preventive and remedial programs. They are treated as recipients of services when they are viewed as creatures to be pitied, 'fixed,' and 'controlled'."

Hooray for Nathan and Kielsmeier. They, along with many others, recognize that we—the adult community—must see our young people as valuable resources and producers if we want them to be effective and responsible citizens—that is, if we want them to be of service to us as well as to themselves. Nathan and Kielsmeier have "hit the nail on the head" when it comes to dealing with gangs.

The quickest and most effective way to reach and turn around gang members, as well as, keeping other young people from joining gangs is to treat them as being needed—and then to use them in caring and educationally sound ways to serve their communities.

Fortunately there are now many illustrations of successful student community service programs which have been integrated into curricula. Most of these programs have been instituted in middle class schools, but more than enough of such programs have been tried in low income areas to recognize their value there too.

A growing awareness of this value of community service education is to be seen in the United States in the National and Community Service Act of 1990. This act provided demonstration funds which by and large have facilitated the growth of this concept.

However, it is local organizations and schools and states and provinces where the creative work has been done. This is because no curriculum including community service can be constructed which would be appropriate for every area. According to Nathan and Kielsmeier (1991), fourth through sixth grade students in one of the lowest income area schools in Oregon were responsible for the cleanup of a hazardous waste site, the passage of two environmental

laws, the planting of hundreds of trees and the com-
pletion of a number of neighborhood improvements.

These educators also cite students at a school in
the South Bronx section of New York City who are
working with a local organization to restore a building for the homeless, including some of the students
own families. They cite middle school students in
Massachesetts for saving their town $119,000 while
solving a sewage problem; high school students in
Georgia who conducted a needs assessment of and
for their community which resulted in a program of
day care; middle and high school students in Min-
nesota who worked on 350 real consumer problems
referred to them by adults and helped resolve 75% of
them; and even of 5- to 9-year-old students who for
their community studied, designed, obtained the
material and helped build a new playground.

What did all of these students learn? According
to Nathan and Kielsmeier, they learned to do research, to problem solve, to think, to write, and to
speak in public. That's my experience too, even in
gang infested areas with many gang members participating.

We had a community service program in one of
my schools where many gang members worked as
tutors. I seldom had any problem with these stu-

dents and I had almost no problem in getting them to volunteer. The major problem for me was that I was a long way from providing community service experiences to every one of my students.

I believe that we should institute community service as a required part of every curriculum from the first years of schooling through the last. I believe this first, because I see community service as a practical vehicle for effectively teaching not only the basics of reading, writing, and computing but the basics for thinking, developing knowledge and instilling values of good citizenship.

It strengthens pride and self-esteem. It strengthens compassion and caring. It does what every decent citizen wants for both self and others.

What does it take to produce an effective community service program in our schools. I can speak from experience that in the inner cities where gangs are present, which may well be true for middle class schools too, that the teacher is the critical person. She or he must be provided with the necessary information materials and skills. Referring back to previous discussion, skills in employing cooperative teaching methods must be developed because they make community service education possible. The use of cooperative teaching methods can make community service experiences fruitful, indeed.

11
Epilogue

While wondering what should be included in this epilogue, my mind kept wandering to something I had just heard as I walked into class today. My students were discussing a twelve-year old "hit man." He was the "trigger man" for a gang, and he had just killed one of his gang's enemies. This "hit man" child was being talked about as if he were a hero.

Another comment by a twenty year old member of the "Bloods," one of the largest and toughest street gangs in the nation, then haunted me. He said as he tried to explain why he stayed in his gang, *"You have to go with what you know."* I felt sad for that poor

twenty year old kid who knew of no other viable alternative for self. He wasn't lazy. He didn't lack in
intelligence. However, the only thing he knew how
to do well was to be a "Blood," and all that being a
"Blood" implies. He was going with what he knew.

"Please," I thought, "If our public school system
can be part of the solution, how must it change?
How must we change what our youth know, feel and
value. Have I made the right suggestions?"

Perhaps the suggestions which I have offered
here—which certainly aren't new, except as to their
application—are not right for every circumstance.
Yet these are ways which have worked for me and for
many of my colleagues. They have proven useful in
the four important areas of schooling:

- one on one interaction,

- classroom conduct,

- school climate, and

- school-community interface.

Which level or program do you favor? Of this I
am sure, no single program or effort for working

with gangs will work. It will require many simultaneous efforts applied in all areas of our communities and at all levels of decision making. There must be fundamental changes in the entire way we conduct our schools if we are going to address the alienation, drugs, guns, and violence that exists in our inner city areas. Unless we can reduce the alienation of our inner city youth and their elders— and people everywhere—our democratic culture is going to suffer badly. Our people, rich and poor alike, are going to be the losers.

Our educational delivery system, particularly in the inner cities, must be reformed if we are to be winners. Unfortunately, that reform, if one can call it that, is most likely to come in the private sector by way of politicians who will pander to those parents who see private education as a way of escaping the public schools. Yet there are youth who must or will remain there; they cannot escape. Unless we publically reach hundreds of thousands of these students, we will soon have millions and millions of people whose existence will threaten every aspect of our social, economic and moral order.

Is it asking too much that our inner city schools be changed into places where young people want to be and want to learn, with the help of staff who also want to be there. What we need to do is to reduce the alienation from education that now exists in our inner city communities and schools.

It wouldn't cost that much.

Rather, bonding school staff, students and the community together will save the lives of thousands of inner-city youngsters as well as the untold dollars that would not be needed to maintain our prisons and social welfare programs.

I believe that we can create such bonding in and among our schools and communities. It has been done, and is being done, in a few places. The idea isn't wierd. General Colin L. Powell suggested bonding when he compared certain tasks of education with conducting difficult military operations—he said there must be a "team spirit."

"In our schools, we must teach our children that alone it is difficult to accomplish things but that together, as a team, as a family almost anything can be accomplished."

Source: *The New Perspectives Quarterly,*
"The Continuing American Dilemma."
Colin Powell, Vol. 8, No. 3, p 19, Summer 1991.

BIBLIOGRAPHY

Books

Arnold, Peter. *Crime and Youth.* Julian Messner, NY: 1976.

Bellanca, J. and Fogarty, Robin. *Blueprints for Thinking in the Cooperative Classroom.* Skylight Publishing, Inc., Palantine, IL, 1990.

Bing, Leon. *For the First Time, Members of L.A.'s Most Notorious Teenage Gangs — The Crips & the Bloods Speak for Themselves.* Harper Collins Publishers, Inc., New York City, NY: 1991

Brookover, Wilbur, et al. *Creating Effective Schools.* Learning Publications, Inc., Holmes Beach, FL: 1982.

Campbell Anne. *Girls in the Gang,* 2nd ed. Blackwell, Basil, Inc., New York City, NY: 1991.

Center for Democratic Renewal. *When Hate Groups Come to Town.* Atlanta, GA: 1985.

Dishon, Dee and Pat Wilson. *A Guidebook for Cooperative Learning.* Learning Publications, Inc., Holmes Beach, FL: 1984.

Final Report of the Governor's Task Force on Violence and Extremism. Baltimore, MD: 1987.

Haskins, James. *Street Gangs Yesterday and Today.* Hastings House, NY: 1974.

Jankowski, Martin S. *Islands in the Street: Gangs & American Urban Society.* University of California Press, Berkeley, CA: 1991.

L.A. County Probation Department. *L.A. County Inter-Agency Task Force on Gang Violence,* 1983.

McEvoy, Alan and Edsel Erickson. *Youth and Exploitation.* Learning Publications, Inc., Holmes Beach, FL: 1990.

National School Safety Center. *Gangs in Schools.* Pepperdine University Press, Malibu, CA: 1988.

Olivero, Michael J. *Honor, Violence & Upward Mobility: A Case Study of Chicago Gangs During the 1970's & 1980's.* University of Texas-Pan American Press, Austin, TX: 1991.

Short, James F. *Gang Delinquency and Delinquent Subcultures.* Harper and Row, 1968.

Slaughter, Charles H. *Good Principals, Good Schools*. Learning Publications, Inc., Holmes Beach, FL: 1989.

Stark, Evan. *Everything You Need to Know about Street Gangs*. The Rosen Publishing Group, Inc., New York City, NY: 1991.

U.S. Conference of Mayors. *A Status Report on Children in America's Cities*. Washington, DC: 1988.

U.S. Department of Justice. *Police Handling of Youth Gangs*. 1983.

Van de Kamp, Attorney General, California. *Street Gang Activity*. 1982.

Vigil, James D. *Barrio Gangs: Street Life & Identity in Southern California*. University of Texas Press, Austin, TX: 1988.

Webb, Margot. *Coping with Street Gangs*. The Rosen Publishing Group, Inc., New York City, NY: 1990.

Articles

Arthur, Richard F. "How to help gangs win the self-esteem battle." *School Administrator*, v46 n5, May 1989.

Barich, Bill. "A reporter at large: the crazy life." *The New Yorker*, November 3, 1986.

Bing, Leon. "Do or die: living the gang life with the Bloods and the Crips." *Rolling Stone*, July 11, 1991.

Bing, Leon. "When you're a Crip (or a Blood)." *Harper's Magazine*, March 1989.

Blauvelt, Peter D. "School security: Who you gonna call?" *School Safety*, Fall 1990.

Bosc, Michael. "Street gangs no longer just a big-city problem." *U.S. News & World Report*, July 16, 1984.

Came, Barry. "A growing menace: violent skinheads are raising urban fears." *Maclean's*, January 23, 1989.

Campbell, Anne. "Self definition by rejection: the case of gang girls." *Social Problems*, December 1987.

Campbell, Anne. "Girls talk: the social representation of aggression by female gang members." *Criminal Justice and Behavior*, June 1984.

Curry, David and Spergel, Irving A. "Gang homicide, delinquency, and community." *Criminology*, August 1988.

"Dirty Harry's children." *The Economist*, il v318, January 12, 1991.

Fagan, Jeffrey. "The social organization of drug use and drug dealing among urban gangs." *Criminology*, il v27, November 1989.

Freitag, Michael. "The attraction of the disreputable." *The New York Times Book Review*, February 26, 1989.

Gregor, Anne. "Death among the innocent." *Maclean's*, May 22, 1989.

Harper, Suzanne. "LA's gang-busters—lessons learned." *School Safety*, Fall 1989.

Harrington-Leuker, Donna. "Street gangs are big business—and growing." *Executive Educator*, v12 n7, July 1990.

Haslanger, Phil. "A rival to the gangs." *The Progressive*, October 1986.

Hopper, Columbus B. and Moore, Johnny. "Women in outlaw motorcycle gangs." *Journal of Contemporary Ethnography*, January 1990.

Horowitz, Ruth. "Community tolerance of gang violence." *Social Problems*, December 1987.

Huff, C. Ronald. "Youth gangs and public policy." *Crime and Delinquency*, il v35, October 1989.

Kaihla, Paul. "Imprisoned prostitutes: the gangs run lucrative brothels." *Maclean's*, March 25, 1991.

Lingwall, Jill. "Gangs in Des Moines: getting them to SCAT." *Public Management*, November 1990.

Marcotte, Paul. "Gang megatrial rejected: judge says one trial of up to 29 El Rukns would be too burdensome." *ABA Journal*, February 1991.

Maxson, Cheryl L., Margaret A. Gordon and Malcolm W. Klein. "Differences between gang and nongang homicides." *Criminology*, May 1985.

Menacker, Julius. "Getting tough on school-connected crime in Illinois." *West's Education Law Report*, v51 n2, March 30, 1989.

Middleton, Martha. "El-Rukn members convicted." *The National Law Journal*, December 7, 1987.

Middleton, Martha. "Gang says it just wanted money: U.S. says it was a terrorist plot." *The National Law Journal*, November 2, 1987.

Moore, Joan W. and Vigil, James D. "Chicano gangs: group norms and individual factors related to adult criminality." *A Journal of Chicano Studies*, Fall 1987.

Moriarty, Anthony and Fleming, Thomas, W. "Youth gangs aren't just a big-city problem anymore." *Executive Educator*, v12 n7, July 1990.

Murr, Andrew. "When gangs meet the handicapped." *Newsweek*, May 7, 1990.

Nebgen, Mary. "Safe streets in Tacoma." *American School Board Journal*, v177 n10, October 1990.

Pearson, Geoffrey. "The original Hooligans." *History Today*, May 1984.

Pierce, Donald. "Gang violence...not just a big-city problem." *The Police Chief*, November 1990.

Prophet, Matthew. "Safe schools in Portland." *American School Board Journal*, v177 n10, October 1990.

"Reflections of a gangbanger." Harper's Magazine, August 1988.

Reinhold, Robert. "In the middle of L.A.'s gang warfare." *The New York Time Magazine*, May 22, 1988.

Schwartz, Audrey-James. "Middle-class educational values among Latino gang members in east Los Angeles county high schools." *Urban Education*, v24 n3, October 1989.

Sessions, William S. "Gang violence and organized crime." *The Police Chief*, November 1990.

Shorris, Earl. "Sanctuary for L.A. homeboys: the priest who loves gangsters." *The Nation*, December 18, 1989.

Skalitzky, William G. "Aider and abettor liability, the continuing criminal enterprise, and street gangs:

a new twist in an old war on drugs." *Journal of Criminal Law and Criminology*, Summer 1990.

"A slaughter of innocents." *U.S. News & World Report*, July 10, 1989.

Spaights, Ernest and Simpson, Gloria. "Some unique causes of black suicide." *Psychology: A Quarterly Journal of Human Behavior*, v23 n1, 1986.

Stover, Del. "A new breed of youth gang is on the prowl and a bigger threat than ever." *American School Board Journal*, v173 n8, August 1986.

Takata, Susan R. and Zevitz, Richard G. "Divergent perceptions of group delinquency in a midwestern community." *Youth & Society*, il v21, March 1990.

Thompson, David W. and Jason, Leonard A. "Street gangs and preventive interventions." *Criminal Justice and Behavior*, September 1988.

Tursman, Cindy. "Safeguarding schools against gang warfare." *School Administrator*, v46 n5, May 1989.

Walker, Lou Ann. "Vanilla fires: rejected by a hearing world, a deaf gang finds brotherhood and protection on New York's streets." *People Weekly*, July 12, 1982.

Tabor, Mary B.W.   "Police try Beantown comics." *The New York Times*, August 4, 1991.